Counselling People
with
Disfigurement

Eileen Bradbury

Communication and Counselling in Health Care
Series editor: Hilton Davis

Counselling People with Disfigurement

Eileen Bradbury

*Department of Plastic and Reconstructive Surgery,
Withington Hospital, University of Manchester*

BPS
BOOKS Published by The British Psychological Society

First published in 1996 by BPS Books (The British Psychological Society),
St Andrews House, 48 Princess Road East, Leicester LE1 7DR, U.K.

Distributed exclusively in North America by Paul H. Brookes Publishing Co., Inc.,
P.O. Box 10624, Baltimore, Maryland 21285, U.S.A.

A catalogue record for this book is available from the British Library.

ISBN 1 85433 176 0 paperback

Phototypeset by Gem Graphics, Trenance, Mawgan Porth, Cornwall
Printed in Great Britain by BPC Wheatons Ltd, Exeter

OTHER TITLES IN THE SERIES
Counselling Parents of Children with Chronic Illness or Disability
by Hilton Davis
Counselling for Heart Disease by Paul Bennett
Counselling in Obstetrics and Gynaecology by Myra Hunter
Counselling People with Diabetes by Richard Shillitoe

CONTENTS

Preface to the Series

People who suffer chronic disease or disability are confronted by problems that are as much psychological as physical, and involve all members of their family and the wider social network. Psycho-social adaptation is important in its own right, in terms of making necessary changes in life style, altering aspirations or coping with an uncertain future. However, it may also influence the effectiveness of the diagnostic and treatment processes, and hence eventual outcomes.

As a consequence, health care, whether preventive or treatment-oriented, must encompass the psychosocial integrated with the physical, at all phases of the life cycle and at all stages of disease. The basis of this is skilled communication and counselling by all involved in providing services, professionally or voluntarily. Everyone, from the student to the experienced practitioner, can benefit from appropriate training in this area, where the social skills required are complex and uncertain.

Although there is a sizeable research literature related to counselling and communication in the area of health care, specialist texts for training purposes are scarce. The current series was, therefore, conceived as a practical resource for all who work in health services. Each book is concerned with a specific area of health care. The authors have been asked to provide detailed information, from the patient's perspective, about the problems (physical, psychological and social) faced by patients and their families. Each book examines the role of counselling and communication in the process of helping people to come to terms and deal with these problems, and presents usable frameworks as a guide to the helping process. Detailed and practical descriptions of the major qualities, abilities and skills that are required to provide the most effective help for patients are included.

The intention is to stimulate professional and voluntary helpers alike to explore their efforts at supportive communication. It is hoped that by so doing, they become sufficiently aware of patient difficulties and the processes of adaptation, and more able to facilitate positive adjustment. The aims of the series will have been met if patients and their families feel someone has listened and if they feel respected in their struggle for health. A central theme is the effort to make people feel better about themselves and able to face the future, no matter how bleak, with dignity.

Hilton Davis
Series editor

I would like to dedicate this book to my children, Jessica and William. I would also like to acknowledge my debt of gratitude to the people with disfigurement from whom I have learned so much, and to my surgical colleagues who have given me so much encouragement and support.

1

Disfigurement and its Treatment

In this book I will use the word 'disfigurement' to describe a visible malformation of the face, head, hands, or legs which is a *consequence* of a physical condition. It is *not* a condition in itself. There are other parts of the body that can be disfigured, such as a breast following a mastectomy, but the main emphasis of this book is on disfigurement which is immediately visible to others. The word 'disfigurement' carries an emotional impact as it can be used as an insult, and is often distressing for the person involved. However, the stigma lies in the meaning attached to the word by the user, and any other word would soon develop the same stigma; it is not the actual *word* that is at fault, but the *meaning* it has for people. There are no satisfactory substitutes, but words which can hurt should always be used with care, and with an understanding of their potential impact. It is generally unnecessary to use the term 'disfigured' with the person involved – it is more appropriate to talk specifically of the condition. However, the person may well use the word, and others such as 'deformed' or 'abnormal'. The distress and anger which often accompany these words is an indication of their power to hurt.

Those who are disfigured may experience psychological and social problems as a result of their disfigurement, and at times they may need help from others in order to cope with these problems. Help in the medical context is generally seen as physical and practical, but every contact with a professional can also be an opportunity to facilitate the person's general adaptation, to reduce distress or to deal with specific psychological and social problems. The purpose of this book is to provide practical advice for those who wish to offer such help.

What do I mean by a 'helper' in this context? There are three main groups of people who may find this book useful:

• *professionals such as psychologists, counsellors, social workers and specialist nurses* who have training in psychological therapies, but would like to gain some insight into the particular problems of this group of people, and possible strategies for intervention;

- *other professionals such as nurses and doctors,* who have not had training in psychological interventions, but are treating someone with disfigurement, and would like to offer more help to them; and
- *friends and family of those with disfigurement* who wish to understand the problems their friend or family member is facing, and to help where they can.

This book is intended to cover the whole age range, and includes strategies specifically aimed at children, adolescents and adults. In addition, it looks at ways of helping parents of children with disfigurement, and also the child's brothers and sisters, and later their partners.

Causes of Disfigurement

There are three broad categories of disfigurement.

Congenital disfigurement

This is the result of genetic inheritance – early malformation of the genes in foetal development or an accident in the womb. It includes clefts of the lip and palate, facial haemangiomas (birthmarks) and a range of craniofacial and hand conditions. Although it is not always possible to determine the exact cause of the congenital anomaly, it is clear when there is an obvious family history, or when there are signs of an accident in the womb, for example, the loss of fingers because of amniotic bands having been wrapped around them. However, there are also many areas of uncertainty and controversy including the debates on the effects of environmental pollution and on medication taken during pregnancy.

Traumatic disfigurement

This is due to the results of an accident. Disfigurement may have been the result of a devastating house fire in which a person received burns to major areas of their body, or a scald on a baby's skin which has left discoloured and deforming scars. Burns are the main cause of disfigurement for children, whereas adults are more likely to be disfigured as a result of an industrial injury, car accident or assault. Scars can be improved by surgery, but they do not disappear. They leave a permanent reminder to the person and to those they meet that they have been injured.

Disease processes

People of all ages can suffer from diseases which leave them with temporary or permanent disfigurement. This may arise primarily from the disease itself, as in acne scarring or facial nerve palsy. Disfigurement as a result of disease is usually progressive, and it may be a long time before the permanent disfigurement can be seen. Disfigurement can also result from the surgery to treat the disease. This is most obvious in head and neck cancers, where life-saving surgery can lead to the removal of areas of the face. The success of reconstruction depends on the site of surgery and on the amount of tissue and bone removed.

Physical Treatments

Those with disfigurement often have a lot of contact with hospitals and undergo a wide range of treatment. Thus it is worth spending some time considering what sort of physical and surgical treatments the people you are working with may have experienced.

Reconstructive surgery

This is generally carried out by plastic surgeons, who have specialist training in the movement of skin, soft tissue and bone. Plastic surgeons deal with *function* (does the hand move well, does the mouth open widely?), and *appearance*, which includes the *colour* of the scar or the skin), the *contour* of the skin (whether it follows the shape of the face or hand), and the *texture* (how does the skin feel when touched?).The surgeon will make an assessment of what can be done, and will suggest the likely outcome of any surgery. However, they will never offer guarantees as to appearance after the surgery has taken place.

The methods they use include:

Skin grafts. Here skin is taken from one part of the body and placed over an area which needs new skin, as in the case of a burn. The grafted skin remains rather wrinkled, and may be different in colour from the surrounding skin. The donor site, where the skin is taken from, is initially sore and needs protection from the sun. It may remain permanently lighter in colour.

Flaps. In this method, skin and underlying tissue containing blood vessels are moved to another part of the body to fill in a larger area.

Flaps are commonly used following cancer surgery, such as that for head and neck cancer and mastectomies. They leave a greater deficit at the donor site, particularly in its contour.

Tissue expansion. This is a technique where a special type of balloon is inserted surgically under good skin adjacent to the damaged skin. The balloon is expanded with saline solution over a period of weeks (although sometimes this is more rapid) and eventually, when enough skin has been created, the balloon is removed, the damaged skin cut out, and the new skin draped over to cover the area from where the damaged skin has been taken. There is thus a short-term period of increasing deformity as the expander grows in size, and a final result which leaves fine scars where the new skin has been stitched into place. This technique is particularly effective for hairy facial birth marks and for loss of hair to the scalp following burns. It is also used following mastectomy, in order to expand up the skin on the chest wall so that a breast implant can be inserted.

Craniofacial reconstruction. This is when the bones of the skull are re-arranged and altered in order to improve the shape of the skull and give it a more normal appearance. It is often carried out at an early age in order to allow normal brain development to occur, which otherwise might have been affected by the constrictions of the abnormal skull shape. This work is generally carried out at specialist craniofacial centres, and the child is carefully assessed prior to surgery. Immediately following surgery, the deformity is greatly increased, and the child's face is distorted and swollen, although this gradually settles over the next few weeks.

Surgery can be very effective in bringing about changes in appearance, but it is a painful, uncomfortable and often frightening process, and some people undergo many operations to reconstruct the problem area. There are other forms of treatment which can be used in addition to, or instead of, surgery.

Laser therapy

Lasers have been with us for some time, but it is only in recent years that they have been used in this field. There are different sorts of lasers, and the more modern types, such as pulse lasers, can be very effective. The most common use of lasers in the treatment of disfigurement is for discoloured skin, such as port-wine stains, and it is also often used in removing tattoos. The treatment is carried out at specialist centres, usually under the care of a dermatologist or plastic surgeon. Each treatment involves a laser beam being directed at the discoloured part of the skin; the number of treatment sessions depends on the depth of discoloration and the extent of the area. Successful laser therapy can remove all the discoloration from the skin, sometimes without scarring, depending on the condition and the type of laser used, but it is not suitable for every condition.

Cosmetic camouflage

This is a specialist type of beauty therapy where skin discoloration is covered with special types of make-up. It is available in many dermatology departments, and is carried out under the supervision of a beauty therapist and/or the Red Cross. It can be very helpful for those with discoloured areas, such as flat red scars, as it reduces the impact of the colour. It can also be used successfully to cover a birthmark, or loss of skin pigmentation, and its advantage is that it has no side-effects. Some people enjoy using it, and find it helps them deal with their disfigurement in a way that is under their control. Cosmetic camouflage does have its limitations, in that it does not deal with problems of texture and contour, and it can take a long time to apply. It is less suitable for males, who quite reasonably feel that others can see it.

Prosthetics

These are artificial parts which are used to replace body parts that may have been missing from birth, or lost following disease or surgery. Areas which can be successfully replaced by prosthetics include eyes, jaws, hands and legs. The prostheses are made of materials such as plastic and metal and are intended to resemble as closely as possible the missing body part, which is particularly important for the face. Prosthetics are used where reconstructive surgery is not possible, and also when the person does not want to go through the process of such surgery.

Artificial arms may be purely functional, with hooks and tools, or purely cosmetic to look like a hand but having no movement. Recent technology has led to the production of biomechanical arms which work on batteries and combine function with a reasonable cosmetic appearance. The work is carried out at the Artificial Limb Centre (or ALAC), under the guidance of a consultant in rehabilitation, and with occupational therapists or physiotherapists. An artificial arm can be very effective when fitted from an early age, as the child grows up with it. However, children may go through stages when they will reject it and refuse to wear it. This is usually a passing phase, and the child will use the arm again when he or she feels the need.

Professionals Involved in the Treatment of Disfigurement

The parents of a baby born with a congenital disfigurement, or the person who acquires a disfigurement may suddenly be confronted by a wide range of professionals. The following is a brief list of those professionals whom the person may meet in the course of treatment for their condition or disfigurement.

Plastic surgeons. These are medically qualified personnel who have trained as surgeons and then have specialized in plastic surgery. They have a long and intensive training in the surgical movement of skin and other tissue, and often specialize in one particular area of plastic surgery.

Oral surgeons. These are trained surgeons who have specialized in the area of surgery to the bones of the skull, in particular, the jaw and neck. They are likely to be involved in carrying out surgery where the alignment of the jaw needs to be changed, for example, when the lower jaw protrudes too far.

Orthodontists. These are medical personnel who have trained as dentists and have then had specialized training in the movement of teeth and the complex problems of dentistry. They generally work at dental hospitals.

Dermatologists. These are physicians who deal with skin conditions which need medical treatment. These conditions include acne, eczema, psoriasis, and some skin cancers. They prescribe tablets, creams and lotions, and give advice about management of the skin. They are often involved in the laser treatment described earlier.

Psychologists. These are non-medical professionals who are trained to deal with emotional and behavioural problems which need specialist help. Their training is based on a knowledge of psychological theory followed by specialized clinical training. They generally work with individuals or with families, and they might, for example, be asked to treat someone who needs help in adjusting to altered body image and is suffering a crisis of identity.

Psychiatrists. These are doctors who have specialized in the field of psychiatry and work with people who are experiencing different types of psychiatric illness. For example, they may be called upon to see a patient when there are signs of mental disturbance following a traumatic injury.

Nurses. Everyone is aware of the nurse's role in looking after the physical needs of patients in hospital. However, there are other ways in which nurses can be involved in the care of those with disfigurement. Nurses have daily contact with patients and their families at times of hospital treatment, and thus may be the first professionals to be aware of any distress. Their training now includes counselling skills, and they are often well-placed to offer immediate help. Because they see so many patients in their daily work, they are able to identify patients' reactions to their disfigurement or to traumatic injury which are such that they would benefit from referral to psychology or psychiatry. Specialist services, such as burns units and breast surgery units, may employ nurses whose primary responsibility is to take on this helping role. These nurses tend to liaise between the hospital and community care, while others may work entirely in the community, such as community psychiatric nurses. They generally work within a community health care team and see people in their own homes. Thus the nursing role has expanded and diversified and nurses are particularly well-placed to play an important part in the helping process.

Health visitors. Working closely with the local family doctor, these specialist nurses work in the community, and are involved in the care of babies and young children, although their case-load can include people of any age. Babies born with cleft palate or associated craniofacial anomalies often have feeding problems, and the health visitor plays a particular role in helping the parents with feeding. They are also involved in monitoring the development of young children, and thus have close and regular contact with families where the child's development may be delayed. For example, babies with craniofacial anomalies may have developmental delay. Because health visitors have regular contact with the family in their homes, they may find that they are involved in helping the parents to cope with emotional adjustment to the birth of their baby.

Health visitors may also play a role in the care of patients discharged from hospital who have had surgery to the head and neck and who have problems with eating and general daily functions.

Speech and language therapists. These are professionals who are specifically trained to identify and treat speech and language problems. They become involved when there are speech problems due to conditions such as cleft palate, or following surgery for mouth cancer, and they are also involved in helping with eating and swallowing problems. They will make a detailed assessment, which may be followed by specific advice, or the person may attend a speech therapy department for treatment to help them improve their speech and/or their eating.

Physiotherapists and occupational therapists. These are professionals who are trained in the work of rehabilitation. The physiotherapist works to improve movement while the occupational therapist helps the individual regain general functioning in all aspects of daily life. They generally work within hospital therapy departments.

Genetic counsellors. These are doctors who have a specialist knowledge of particular congenital conditions. They attempt to advise families about the reasons why the congenital deformity may have happened, and what the chances are of it appearing in future generations. They usually like to see all the immediate family, and will carry out various tests, including blood tests, in order to identify genetic factors in the family which may have caused the condition. This can be important for the family in making decisions about having more children, or in advising their child when he or she is older about the risk of producing children with the same condition.

Thus we can see that the problems associated with conditions which cause disfigurement can be many and varied, and care can be wide-ranging. However, before anyone can offer help, they need to understand the problems associated with disfigurement, and to put those problems into a framework of a helping process. Although there are specific issues relating to disfigurement, they should be approached within this broader framework; thus experience in other areas can be carried over and can enrich our understanding of human responses to the stress of disfigurement. Within this book, discussion of disfigurement and of the helping process comes before more detailed descriptions of ways of helping. This book aims to increase your knowledge so that you can be more effective in the help you offer to those with disfigurement.

SUMMARY

Visible disfigurement has a significant impact on the individual affected, the family and society. This book aims to guide those who wish to help people to cope with disfigurement.

❏ There are many causes of disfigurement, although they can be usefully grouped together as follows:
  1. *congenital*, e.g. cleft lip, birthmarks, hand conditions
  2. *traumatic*, e.g. burns, facial scarring
  3. *disease processes*, e.g. head and neck cancer

❏ There are different types of physical treatment to improve disfigurement, and these include:
  1. *reconstructive surgery* (surgery to bone, soft tissue and skin to modify disfigurement)
  2. *laser therapy* (removing pigment from the skin and deep layers)
  3. *cosmetic camouflage* (the use of make-up to cover marks)
  4. *prosthetics* (artificial parts)

❏ Individuals and their families may meet many unfamiliar professionals who will be involved in this treatment. These include:
  1. *Plastic surgeons*
  2. *Oral and maxillo-facial surgeons*
  3. *Orthodontists*
  4. *Dermatologists*
  5. *Psychologists*
  6. *Psychiatrists*
  7. *Nurses*
  8. *Health Visitors*
  9. *Speech and language therapists*
  10. *Physiotherapists and occupational therapists*
  11. *Genetic counsellors*

❏ An understanding of the physical aspects of disfigurement can help both the individual with disfigurement and the helper.

2

The Psychological and Social Effects of Disfigurement

I, that am curtailed of this fair proportion,
Cheated of feature by dissembling Nature,
Deformed, unfinished, sent before my time
Into this breathing world, scarce half made up,
And that so lamely and unfashionable
That dogs bark at me as I halt by them
Richard III (William Shakespeare)

The problems of disfigurement are not new; they have been with us for centuries. Those who look different from others because they have some form of visible disfigurement have long suffered from the responses of others to them, and from their own emotions about their disfigurement. Their physical condition is treated by skilled professionals who reconstruct their faces, hands and legs following devastating injury, or who repair the physical consequences of a congenital problem like a cleft lip. However, their emotional responses to their disfigurement are not always understood, and there has been very little practical guidance for those who wish to help people cope with their sense of difference.

What are the Problems faced by People with Disfigurement?

Those with visible disfigurement may experience any of the following psychological and social problems because of their disfigurement.

Difficulties in social encounters: the responses of strangers

Those with major disfigurement are often a hidden population. Despite the high incidence of facial burns and other types of facial disfigurement, we do not see many people with noticeable disfigurement walking down the High Street. The experience of people with disfigurement when they do go out can be very difficult. I sat in the choir stalls of York Minster for choral evensong behind a friend with major disfigurement. The people around me were staring at him intently. Walking down the street with someone who is disfigured, you become aware of the reaction of others and of the staring, the pointing and the whispered comments. People with disfigurement describe this as a loss of privacy as others put normal social rules to one side. Staring is felt to be a hostile activity, robbing the person who is stared at of dignity and humanity. It is the most common social response to disfigurement and can lead the person with disfigurement to avoid social situations. When they do go out, they often become hyper-vigilant and watch others to see if they are staring. This is particularly true for parents of children with disfigurement who describe a continued state of tension of feeling like a 'clenched fist'. Sometimes strangers who stare are confronted by them, and this state of hyper-vigilance can be very exhausting.

Some people with disfigurement do experience genuine hostility from strangers. There is an adolescent girl I know who was badly burned in a house fire many years ago. She travels on public transport with a Sony Walkman so that she does not hear the comments and the names she gets called, such as 'Freddy Kruger'. Another man who had facial cancer described how he was attacked by a group of young men, who jeered at his appearance.

The third major social response can be *avoidance*. When I took a young client of mine to the local fast-food restaurant, we both became aware that the woman at the till would not look at her but addressed all her comments to me, even though the girl did the ordering. People with disfigurement describe how strangers sometimes seem embar-rassed and cannot meet their eye. This makes it difficult to carry on any conversation or to break through social barriers.

Disruption to normal patterns of work and play

Because of the problems described in social encounters, many people with disfigurement may exclude themselves from normal social activities. In addition, prolonged hospitalization and further treatment can have an effect, and this can be of crucial importance for children. They find that their problems at school are compounded by the interruptions to their education. Following a serious burn, children can spend several months in hospital and at home. There then follows many operations and visits to hospital. If these are timed for school holidays, the children may find that they miss out on social activities with friends and family. If hospital treatment happens during school-time, then they miss out on their education. They also may find that their concentration at school is affected by their disturbed emotional state and by any difficulties in relationships with the other children. Loss of time at school also means loss of social time with other children. Hospital becomes a safe haven and the children may respond more readily to professionals than to other children. All this can add up to a significant loss of normal patterns of educational and social development which can be as important a disability as the actual physical consequences of the injury.

Adults may also miss out on time at work. Following the original injury and hospitalization, there is the further interruption of hospital visits and admissions. Employers may be less tolerant of absences than schools, and the person with disfigurement may feel that the job has become precarious. In addition, promotion becomes more problematic as it is easier to stay in familiar surroundings because of a fear of others' responses. Interviews for new jobs can be fraught as the person is acutely self-conscious about his or her appearance and finds it difficult to face the interviewers, and so their aspirations may be modified. For example, Goldberg (1974) compared a group of adolescents handicapped by a serious heart condition with a group with facial disfigurement. He found that those with heart problems had higher career aspirations despite their health problems. Thus disfigurement can have consequences in terms of work as well as education.

Disruption to body image

We are familiar with our appearance from an early age, and learn the effect our appearance has on other people. Following an abrupt change in appearance due to trauma, disease and/or surgery, looking into the mirror and failing to recognize the face looking back can be a crisis. Parents search the face of their child to find the child they knew before. Identity is bound up with appearance, and those with disfigurement can lose their sense of self, and also their family identity, their gender identity and their racial identity. Family identity is lost as the person no longer looks like parents, grandparents, siblings and/or children. Gender identity can be lost when a man feels emasculated by a debilitating hand injury, or a woman feels less feminine because of major facial scars, and racial identity can be lost following burns when the dark pigment in the skin is destroyed. This perception of loss of identity can lead to anxiety and depression, to feelings of isolation and to a grieving response for the identity which has been lost.

These feelings are not confined to those with traumatic injury. Parents of children born with congenital disfigurement describe their sadness that the baby does not look like them. A child with a major craniofacial condition such as Apert's syndrome, with a high skull and flattened features, looks more like other children with Apert's than his or her family. This may make it harder for some parents to accept the child as truly their own. Adults with congenital disfigurement have described to me a sense of being 'haunted by ghosts' – the ghost of the person they would have been if they had not had the condition.

Self-consciousness. The disruption to body image and difficulties in social encounters can lead to a sense of self-consciousness. Whether the disfigurement has been congenital or traumatic, both children and adults can feel very self-conscious about their appearance. This is characterized by an increased focus on the features which are disfigured, so that they become the most significant aspect of the person's appearance to them. They assume that this is the first thing anyone sees, and that others are making judgements because of these features. This may result in a feeling of shame and the need to hide the part as much as possible. Hair is pulled over the face, dark glasses are worn, the head is kept down. Those who are self-conscious about their hands keep them in their pockets away from the view of others and of themselves. This covering up and concealment can feel precarious and the person may feel the need to constantly check that the hair or the glasses are in place. This can also happen with concealing make-up.

Self-consciousness and feelings of shame about one's body can cause sexual problems and can have an impact on an existing sexual relationship. For example, sexual problems following hand injury are common, as the hand may lose its sensitivity and ability to touch and caress in the same way as before, and the partner may feel uncomfortable with the altered touch. There can also be problems in forming new relationships. The person with facial disfigurement may have no confidence in kissing, and burns to the body can cause someone to feel hesitant about exposing their body. Those with disfigurement often say that they feel less sexually attractive than others, and this can be a major problem for them.

Coping with treatment and decision-making about treatment

Those with visible disfigurement will often have to deal with treatment to improve their condition, and the types of treatment they may come across have been described in Chapter 1. There are two aspects to be taken into consideration: deciding whether or not to have treatment, and coping with it when it takes place. Decision-making about surgery can cause problems if the individual or family feels that they do not have enough information to make a decision, that they have not been listened to in the clinic or that their emotional state makes any such decision difficult. It is particularly difficult for parents to make decisions on behalf of their children, as they have to attempt to anticipate the child's needs as an adult (Bradbury *et al.*, 1994b).

Treatment itself can be worrying, painful and time-consuming. The outcome is often uncertain, and lack of preparation may leave the individual and family disappointed with the result. Parents of children with disfigurement may find that reconstructive surgery helps them adjust to their child's situation as they feel that they are doing what they can to improve the child's appearance. This helps reduce the sense of guilt and responsibility many parents feel. However, research has shown that children do not always benefit as much as their parents from surgery, particularly if they were having considerable social difficulties before the operation (Bradbury *et al.*, 1994c). The factors which influence outcome often relate to the person's psychological and social state rather than to the technical quality of the surgical result (Bradbury *et al.*, 1992).

Post-traumatic stress

Those who have suffered traumatic disfigurement may also suffer from symptoms of post-traumatic stress. Many of these symptoms arise because of the traumatic nature of the injury. Those who have had a frightening experience of injury, particularly if they thought they were going to die, often describe having vivid nightmares and flashbacks (suddenly visualizing the accident whilst awake). These are generally intrusive and disturbing to the individual, who may feel that he or she is 'going mad'. However, re-experiencing the events of a traumatic injury is a very common reaction and generally passes with time. Reminders of the event, such as seeing similar accidents on television, can trigger further flashbacks and nightmares. The person may find this so distressing that any reminders are avoided. And this can cause problems in returning to work. The sight of the disfigured part itself may act as the trigger, and this can cause the person to avoid looking at it – it is not unusual to find a person with a hand injury keeping his or her hand covered up and having difficulty looking at the damaged hand because it brings back disturbing and intrusive memories.

There are also frequently signs of mood disturbance, such as irritability and poor concentration. The mood changes tend to persist for some time and can be compounded by anxiety about treatment, frustration with slow physical recovery, financial worries and boredom if the person cannot get back to work. Those close to the person may find all this difficult to tolerate, particularly if the moods continue for a long time. Occasionally, when severe symptoms do persist, the person may need psychological or psychiatric help.

Parental adjustment to the birth

When parents have problems in adjusting to their child's disfigurement, they often display characteristic signs which can alert the helper to the extent of the problem. These are:

The length of overt grieving and distress. Parents who continue to show strong emotional responses such as distress or anger which dominate their emotional state months and years after the onset of the condition have not resolved their grieving for the 'perfect' child.

Taking the baby/child out. It is important to identify whether this is an area of difficulty. Responses can range from taking the child out and about without any anxiety to avoiding taking the child out at all unless covered up. Many parents fall in between, and 'guard the pram' by speaking first to people who come to look or by doing battle with them.

The taking and displaying of photos. Some parents find it very difficult to take and/or display photos of their child, so that the child growing up may feel unaccepted and unacceptable. It also means there is no record of their childhood.

Responses to surgery. Surgery and other treatment to correct the problem may be seen by some parents as crucial to their acceptance of their child. Attachment may be withheld until surgery takes place.

Decisions to have further children. Parents who are devastated by having a child with a physical imperfection may feel that they cannot risk having another child because the condition is too overwhelming for them. Other parents feel that they have to have another child straight away in order to prove to themselves and others that they can have a normal child. Many others require detailed scans and reassurance. The ability of the parents to tolerate the thought of having a child with the same condition indicates how much it has affected them.

Effect on the marital partnership. Many parents draw together in adversity, but some relationships may be put under strain as the partners are not moving forward in synchrony and may misunderstand each other's responses. If the father has to act as the conduit to the outside world and needs information, he may also be more comfortable in that role in any case and take it on. He may also feel that he cannot show his emotions because he needs to support his partner, and thus they may respond differently. For some relationships, which are already unstable or under strain, the event may cause the parents to separate.

The length of time it takes to adjust to the new baby varies widely: for some parents, it is a matter of moments; for others, the adjustment difficulties go on for years. The support that parents receive from their families and friends can crucially influence this process (Bradbury and Hewison, 1994a), and this will be considered next.

The responses of family and friends

Those with disfigurement sometimes describe difficulties in close relationships with family, friends and acquaintances. People experiencing traumatic disfigurement may have to cope with the emotions of their family as well as their own emotional responses. For example, a severe burn injury is experienced in different ways by the *whole* family. Parents may suffer feelings of guilt and depression, siblings may become over-protective, or conversely, be ashamed of their brother or sister's appearance. I worked with one family where the younger sister refused to look at her older sister who had been burned, saying that she was not her sister but a 'monster'. Children may find that normal family patterns disappear, as everyone is behaving differently; discipline changes as they find they can get away with anything, and strange adults take over from their parents in hospital and in the community. For some children, these changes are more unsettling and disturbing than the physical consequences of the accident, and can lead to 'naughty' behaviour as they try to establish how far they can go. Children can also be very protective of their parents and become reluctant to say how they feel in case it upsets them.

For those with congenital conditions, the parental and family responses following the birth can be intense and may endure over many years. Difficulties in adjusting to the child may cause the parents to become very distressed and can lead to avoiding others as that is easier than having to deal with others' reactions every time they go out.

Children in the playground may be teased by their peers because of their appearance. Other children may respond with avoidance or hostility, and children with facial disfigurement often report name-calling by others. This can lead to social withdrawal and increased anxiety as the child feels victimized and isolated and potential friends keep their distance because they do not want to be stigmatized by association. Adults who have suffered a traumatic disfigurement often say that they avoid acquaintances who knew them before the accident because it is hard to cope with their shocked and/or pitying responses. They also find it difficult to have to keep explaining what has happened, as talking about it can be very upsetting.

Coping with the media

This is a potential issue for people who are disfigured. A child or adult with a visible disfigurement can become a source of interest to the media, especially if the person has been attacked by a dog or an assailant, or was involved in some disaster. The local media may well descend on any 'human interest story'.

Those who have just experienced a crisis are not best placed to protect themselves against the intrusion of the media. I observed the effect on a boy who was recruited to a 'fly-on-the-wall' hospital documentary after having his arm replanted following traumatic amputation (Bradbury and Kay, 1990). We found that although the boy rather enjoyed some of the attention focused on him, the experience left him with a feeling of being left behind once the attention was past, and the sight of his arm being replanted may well have interfered with the re-integration of his body image. The story told by the media is only one version of reality, and generally the most sensational.

These are some of the common problems experienced by those with disfigurement. In order to fully understand these problems, it is important to understand the historical and cultural factors which influence them.

The Historical and Cultural Context

Disfigurement has long been seen as a form of punishment. Throughout history, criminals have been deliberately disfigured to mark them for all to see. The word *stigma* was first used by the ancient Greeks to describe this process. Even today, there are parts of the world where criminals are punished by having a hand cut off, or by having a tattoo put on their face.

Birth anomalies were traditionally seen as having particular significance. In some societies, they were seen as a sign of the anger of the gods, because of the sins of the parents or the community. Babies born with congenital anomalies were killed to assuage the god's anger, and their mothers often killed with them. Mothers have often been seen as responsible – in many languages, 'birthmark' translates as 'mother's mark'. For example, the cleft or 'hare' lip has a long and complex mythology. It was assumed that the mother had seen a hare, the witches' familiar, and a sign of the devil, when she was pregnant. There was a belief that she had a sexual relationship with the devil resulting in a baby with a lip which looked like the hare's lip. Until this century, butchers in Norway were forbidden by law from hanging hares in their windows in case a pregnant woman saw them. Even today in Northern Norway, some butchers cover the hare's face, although they may no longer know why. This has long given those with such a deformity a terrible sense of visibility and stigma, especially before lips were routinely repaired:

> *All on a sudden I knew that all these folk, the grand ones within and the old fellows without, were staring at my hare-shotten lip.*
>
> (Prudence Sarn in *Precious Bane* by Mary Webb)

There are other beliefs about congenital deformity, as people over the centuries have tried to understand and explain what they find frightening and inexplicable. There is the 'hybrid' creature, the child with large hairy birthmarks or severe craniofacial deformities, which was explained by blaming mothers for having a relationship with an animal. Then there was a belief in the changeling creature, who was not human but who had been substituted for a real baby by the fairies or evil spirits (Shaw, 1981).

This is not all past history. There are also some people who continue to believe these myths. Some people say that a strawberry birthmark means that the mother ate strawberries when she was pregnant, and within some cultures, there are clear and strongly believed reasons for the birth deformity. I visited a Muslim family where a new baby had been born with a severe cleft lip. The mother told me that she knew why it had happened. When pregnant, she had been chopping vegetables one night when there was a full moon. She believed that the chopping action of the knife had caused the cleft lip, which has the appearance of a cut. She was unhappy that it was her fault, but knew that she would never do this again and thus felt that she had some control over the situation.

People have an overwhelming need to find significant reasons for events for which there may be no obvious cause. There is evidence in the literature (Seligman, 1975) that people feel less helpless when they can find a cause – it increases their feelings of control over the situation. They can then predict whether it will happen in the future, and therefore may feel that they have the potential to prevent it occurring again.

Why do people continue to find disfigurement so upsetting? Is it because people who are disfigured may look ugly? Extensive research into the field of physical attractiveness has shown that the attractive child is rated as being more popular than others by their classmates (Dion and Berscheid, 1974), and they receive more attention from the teacher (Langlois and Stephan, 1981). People attribute positive qualities of personality to those who are attractive, and negative qualities to the unattractive.

What is beautiful is good
(Sappho, fragment 101, Dion *et al.*, 1972)

There are also certain facial features, such as a lowering brow or a jutting jaw, which can be perceived as threatening. This type of visual shorthand is widely used in the television and film industry.

However, there is another dimension to disfigurement. The face or hand which is seen as distorted, disfigured or in some way abnormal can evoke fear and avoidance. Social responses to disfigurement have been widely researched (Bull and Rumsey, 1988), and experiments have shown that people will maintain a greater social distance from a disfigured stranger than from a stranger with no visible disfigurement. The emotional responses to disfigurement are stronger than emotional responses to ugliness, and may be essentially different. While reactions to ugliness may include disdain, or feelings of possible physical threat, reactions to disfigurement may be driven by embarrassment and anxiety which can translate into hostility and fear.

The theory of stigma as described by Goffman (1963) gives some insight into characteristic social responses to disfigurement. He discusses the way in which the stigmatized are treated as a stereotyped and discredited sub-group in society. This is based on assumptions that are made about the causes of disfigurement, such as culpability for burns in terms of neglect, or scars resulting from fighting. The stigmatized may strive to hide the stigma in order to reduce their visibility and pass as normal, but visible disfigurement can be very hard to hide. People who feel stigmatized by their disfigured hand may keep it in their pocket, and the facially disfigured may try to use their hair-style, make-up and glasses to minimize the disfigurement. The power of the stigma lies in its acceptance by those who are stigmatized. They are part of our society and therefore understand the social and cultural factors which shape the stigma. Thus there is also an element of self-stigmatization.

The social impact of disfigurement can be reinforced by the negative images of the disfigured portrayed through literature and the media, such as Freddie Kruger in *Nightmare on Elm Street*, the Walt Disney films (for example, the Beast in *Beauty and the Beast*), or in the children's stories of Roald Dahl. I know of one lady with a distorted lip who was distressed to think she was just like the witch in Dahl's *The Witches*. A disfigured face is often used to indicate evil or torment, whilst a beautiful face is often perceived as good; think, for example, of the stepmother and Snow White.

These are some of the social and cultural stressors which may affect the individual with disfigurement. However, not all individuals who experience disfigurement respond in the same way, and there are factors to consider which will influence the individual response of those who experience disfigurement.

Factors which Mediate Individual Responses

This section focuses on factors which interact with the social and cultural stressors described in the previous section. They include common factors such as the effect of age and the effect of the severity and type of disfigurement, and individual factors such as personality, previous experiences and the amount of family and social support.

The effect of age

Children are not born knowing that they are disfigured; this is a gradual process of learning for them. Small babies can recognize others' faces from the early weeks, and will focus more intently on familiar adults, especially their mother. However, it is not until after about 12 months that they start to recognize themselves in a mirror. Babies of 15 months will notice a mark drawn on their face, and will focus on it, so it seems that babies are able to recognize their own faces, and any differences in their faces before they can really talk.

Small babies often lie on their back with their hands in front of their face, and parents report that babies with a hand deficit will focus on the deficient hand more than the other, normal hand. However, it is of crucial importance to recognize that the child's awareness of the discrepancy does not necessarily mean that they are concerned by it. Parents need this reassurance, as they may be waiting with some dread for the child to become aware of their disfigurement and be very troubled when the child shows that they are.

The development of self-consciousness. The development of self-consciousness is both a cognitive and a social process. Cognitively, the child will begin to understand that their face or hand is different from other people's, and that this is part of them. Socially, the child will begin to be aware that other people notice the deformity, and may respond to it in a negative way. In one study (Fisk *et al.*, 1985), children between the ages of four and seven years old were shown pictures of children with a range of facial and body characteristics, and they were asked to choose which children they would like to have as a friend. They were also asked to say what they thought of all the children. Children as young as four rated the children with disfigurement as having negative personality qualities, and these children were ranked with an obese child as the least often chosen as a friend. Thus there is a social response on the part of other children to the disfigured child, and this tends to become clear to the child when they have to leave the protection of home and enter school.

Tanya started school in the local town at the age of five. Her mother had not taken her to nursery because she was worried about how other children would react to her obvious facial disfigurement (the little girl had a red birthmark covering her face). The other children were inclined to keep their distance, and Tanya came home one day in tears because a little boy had called her names. Tanya tended to keep her face down, and would not speak to other people. She felt ashamed of her face, and tried to hide it. This little girl had been influenced by her mother's anxiety in the development of her feelings of self-consciousness about her appearance. Once she went to school, the reactions of other children increased these feelings and led her to develop concealing and avoiding behaviour.

However, this is not an inevitable process, and starting school can be made easier if the other children are familiar with the child. Many of their responses may result from fear and uncertainty with the unfamiliar. Robert lived in a small village, and had always played with the other children. He had a craniofacial malformation, which had left him with a high forehead and protruding eyes. He went to the local nursery and moved up to school with his friends. When a new child called him names, the other children defended him.

Other issues tend to arise between the ages of seven and nine years old. By this age, the child has become aware that the disfigurement will not fade, and there is no magic (including surgery) that will dispel it. This can lead to the child grieving for the loss of the perfect face or hand they never had. This response can manifest itself as outbursts of difficult and uncharacteristic behaviour, sadness and tearfulness, bed-wetting or withdrawn behaviour, made all the more difficult by the child's social development at this age. Children need to be accepted by their peers, and appearance is often a factor of major importance in this. This is the age when children first make demands to wear particular clothes so as to look like everyone else. Children also tend to form themselves into groups at this age and this feeling of group cohesion is often cemented by attacking those not in the group.

It is at this age that children can suffer most from teasing. Nearly all children experience derogatory comments at some time, but for the disfigured child, teasing can increase feelings of helplessness and of being an outsider. This may be reinforced by the responses of the parents, who may have been expecting this from the time the baby was born, especially if they experienced teasing or rejection themselves as children. They may respond to their child's distress with anger or distress themselves, and strategies for dealing with this will be discussed in Chapter 5.

Early adolescence. The next time which can be difficult for the child is early adolescence. This often coincides with a change of school, where the child is exposed to a new, more competitive and less protected environment. At the same time, the child's body image is changing and unstable, and the dissatisfaction many adolescents feel about their bodies can be more intense for those with visible deformity. It can be a very lonely time, especially if the adolescent has not developed close confiding friendships. The family becomes less important than friends at this time, and cannot substitute for them. It is important for the adolescent to be able to separate from the family, but lack of friends, lack of self-confidence, a fear of the outside world and over-protectiveness on the part of parents may all conspire to keep the adolescent dependent on the family.

During this time the adolescent is developing sexual awareness, but the process of dating is more difficult. Nathalie talked about her feelings about boyfriends – all her friends were going out with someone. However, she did not like going to night-clubs because people stared at her burnt face. She felt ugly, and could not imagine approaching anyone. She could not accept her own appearance, and believed that no boy could ever accept her. Some girls I have known have become promiscuous, in a desperate effort to feel accepted by others. All they gained was a reputation for being 'an easy lay'.

Development does not end with adolescence, but continues throughout a person's life. Rutter and Rutter (1992) talk about development as a life-long process with continuities and discontinuities. When young people leave school or further education, they enter the world of work. For some, this can be traumatic, as they move away from a familiar and protected environment to one in which there is a lot of competition, and their appearance can influence their chances on the job market. In addition, if they are self-conscious and ashamed of their appearance, they may lack the confidence to go for jobs which reflect their ability or interest, and look for jobs where they are less visible to others. However, success at work can help a person deal with their self-consciousness. Letitia went to work for a bank on leaving school. Although she was rather shy, she soon showed a flair for the work, and was encouraged to go for further training, and to seek promotion. She said that she never thought about her disfigured face at work, because she was confident in her role there, and felt a sense of authority.

Adulthood

Early adulthood is a busy time, with work, the development of a marriage or partnership, and sometimes children. All these factors can help a person to feel accepted and useful, and this is often a time of growing self-confidence. However, for some, the responses of their children's friends bring a painful reminder of the fact of their disfigurement. Alice had a facial palsy which caused the right side of her face to droop. She had a five-year-old son whom she collected from school each day. One day, his friend came up and asked her why she had a 'twisted face'. She was devastated.

For some people, adulthood brings a reduction of self-consciousness and a growing acceptance that their disfigurement is part of them. Close and stable relationships, and success in other ways can help this process. There may continue to be reminders and comments, and they may still have to deal with stares and nudges, but they can learn to cope with this. However, there may be times when even the most capable and confident person needs help with the coping process. This is particularly true at times of change and stress, such as a change of job, the break-up of a relationship, or when their own children start to ask questions.

I have talked with people who have reached retirement age, and who have expressed the need to share their feelings with someone else. The ability to cope can bring with it the tyranny of always being seen as being strong, and it makes it so much more difficult for those who seem to cope well to admit to having problems. Researchers have found that those who have something visibly different about them can be very defensive, and find it very difficult to admit to any problems (Pillemer and Kay, 1989). The development of self-consciousness is a life-time process of coping and adaptation and it is important never to assume that the process is complete.

The effect of the type of disfigurement

The severity of the disfigurement. It would seem logical to assume that the more severe the disfigurement, the more distress the person will feel. However, those who work in the field know that this is not necessarily the case, and may be puzzled by the levels of distress expressed by someone with what would be classed as a minor disfigurement.

Macgregor (1982), has pointed out that those with more minor disfigurements may well experience great distress. This is linked to the feeling of being in control. When a person has a major burn to the face, they can generally predict the range of responses to this, such as aversion or pity, and thus they can learn ways of dealing with these responses. They may also feel a sense of injustice that others should respond to them in this way, and feel that more respect should be paid to their own feelings.

However, when a person has a minor disfigurement, particularly when that affects the movement of the face such as hemifacial palsy, then the problems can be different. Lucy was a pretty girl in her early twenties who had had Bell's Palsy when she was young. It had left her with a slight droop to the left side of her face, which was more apparent when she smiled and talked. It also felt different to her, as the sensation was altered and rather numb. She was acutely self-conscious about it, and tried to keep her face as still as possible, thus gaining a reputation for being rather miserable and unresponsive. When she did talk to people she found that they tended to focus for a while on the left side of her face. She felt that she could not talk about it, as that would draw attention to it.

When the disfigurement is obvious, other people can make sense of it quickly and then look away. Because the cause of Lucy's disfigurement was not immediately obvious to those who looked at her, they scanned her face more closely in order to make sense of the difference in her face. Her feeling of being stared at was real. However, although those with minor disfigurement may experience more intense staring by others, they may feel that they are making a fuss about nothing. They see people at the hospital and on television with more serious problems and feel rather ashamed of their reactions. They do not feel entitled to make a fuss, although their social experience can be as difficult for them as the experience of people with major disfigurement, and their family may be unsupportive and minimize the problem. Because they cannot predict what others think of their face, or whether they have noticed the disfigurement, they may feel less in control of the situation. Lansdown (1990) described how this feeling of lack of control can cause the person with a minor disfigurement to feel very anxious.

Those with a minor disfigurement may feel wretched because they cannot predict the reactions of others, because of the increased staring of others, because talking about the disfigurement draws attention to it, because there may be lack of family support and because of feelings of shame at their own reactions.

The type and the location of the disfigurement. We do not know enough about the impact of particular types of disfigurement. My own research compared the parents of babies with facial disfigurement (cleft lip) with parents of babies with hand disfigurement (missing fingers and/or small hands and arms) (Bradbury and Hewison, 1994a). There were no differences between the two sets of parents in terms of their adjustment to the baby. It therefore seems to be the fact of having a baby with a disfigurement rather than the type of disfigurement which is most important for parents. However, the older children with clefts in our study were less socially competent, and rather more shy and family-dependent than those with hand problems. This might indicate that a facial problem for the growing child is more worrying than a hand problem.

The closer a disfigurement is to the centres of facial communication – the eyes and the mouth – the more impact it seems to have (Goffman, 1963). A scar which distorts the lip slightly will be more obvious to everyone than a larger scar on the margins of the face.

This also applies to hands. We use our hands in gesture and non-verbal communication, and if someone is self-conscious about the appearance of their hand, and hides it, then they become constrained in their communication. It is also more difficult to touch someone in greeting, such as a hand-shake, or to touch them in an intimate way. The difficulties caused to someone in their daily life by feelings of shame about their hand should not be under-estimated. It should also be realized that whilst a person can avoid their own face by not looking in a mirror, their hand is always in front of them, and it is much more difficult to avoid. However, this can help to facilitate adjustment, as it encourages de-sensitization and can help the re-integration of the damaged part into the body image.

There are other sites of visible disfigurement which may have a particular meaning for people. Pauline was a girl in her late teens. She was involved in a road traffic accident and her leg was badly fractured. She was left with a distorted leg shape, with part of her calf muscle missing, and the front of her leg badly scarred. She refused to look at her leg when the nurses changed the dressings, and begged them to keep it covered. She would not co-operate with any rehabilitation, but became depressed and withdrawn. She had always taken a great pride in her legs, which she considered her best feature, and always wore short skirts to show them off. She could not imagine how she would now cope, and said that she would always wear trousers from now on. Any disfigurement which is visible to others can have an impact on the individual, and the site does need to be considered in understanding that impact.

The meaning of the disfigurement. Those who are disfigured may be profoundly influenced by the beliefs they hold about the meaning others ascribe to their disfigurement. Sometimes these beliefs are based on a realistic appraisal of the situation. Young men who have facial scarring frequently describe how they are turned away from night-clubs and pubs because they are seen as 'trouble'. They also find that they are more likely to get into fights as others 'square up' to them and challenge them; others may believe they have received their scars from fighting, and this influences their social responses. (This is similar to the experience of those with visible tattoos, when others judge them as being 'rough' because of the tattoos. I talked with one man who had tattoos on his hand, who would not go to his son's parents' evening at school, because he felt that the teachers would despise him because of the tattoos and that would affect their reactions to his son.)

Sometimes the meaning the disfigurement has for those with disfigurement is based on cultural beliefs, as already described (p. 18). A person with a hairy birth-mark may believe that others see something animal-like in that mark and consequently treat him or her as less than human.

There are also those who ascribe meanings to disfigurement which are based on individual emotional reactions rather than on social reality. Julie was a rather chaotic little girl who always managed to get her clothes torn and dirty and who had a cheerful and noisy approach to life. Her mother brought her to the dermatologist because of her concern about patches of visible red veins on her cheeks. The child was completely untroubled about these but her mother felt distressed whenever she looked at her. To the mother, these veins represented the way in which the child seemed out of control. The mother was an anxious and rather obsessive person. She eventually agreed that she needed help rather than her daughter. In this case, the meaning the marks had for Julie's mother affected her responses to them, but others did not respond in the same way. Understanding the meaning it has for the person is of vital importance in understanding that person's behaviour. That meaning is usually expressed in terms of beliefs about what they think other people will think when they see the disfigurement.

Congenital and traumatic disfigurement. Is the experience of disfigurement the same for the person who was born with it, as it is for the person who acquires it through accident or disease? When someone is born with disfigurement, their early social experiences will generally be affected by the fact of the disfigurement. Thus the stranger looking into the pram and seeing a child with a serious facial cleft will withhold immediate approval until they have adjusted to the sight of the face. The mother may find it more difficult to respond to the baby's gurgling with responsive noises and smiling if she feels unhappy about the face (Field and Vegha-Lahr, 1984). The child may learn at an early age not to become the centre of attention, as the responses of others may be ambivalent and troubling. Social reactions of other children can be questioning, curious or rejecting. In other words, the child with an obvious disfigurement grows up with an awareness of being different, and this may lead to a sense of being too visible to others. The child may be quieter and may not compete very hard; on the other hand, it may lead the child to compensate for the disfigurement by trying to prove themselves in other ways (Timberlake, 1985).

People who acquire disfigurement are faced with a different adaptation task. They have not grown up with stares and comments or being treated as 'different' and will have developed varying degrees of personal confidence in themselves. However, disfigurement brings with it an abrupt disruption of life, to which people respond differently, and some may have no way of dealing with this. In addition, their body image may have been disrupted, and they may not recognize themselves in a mirror. The sensations in the disfigured area are different and it does not feel or look like part of them. However, because they have grown up unaffected by a sense of looking different from others, they have not been subject to early adverse reactions of others and thus may have a greater confidence in their social acceptability.

It is important to recognize that for both types of disfigurement, congenital and traumatic, there is usually a period of adjustment. This is more obvious for those with traumatic disfigurement. People may mourn the loss of their normal face, hand, leg, or other body part in a similar way to those who are bereaved. As they adjust to their different appearance there may be shock and denial, anger, sadness and then a gradual resolution, as they come to accept that this is indeed themselves.

Those with congenital disfigurement may also experience a period of mourning. One woman told me that she was preoccupied by feelings of loss for the person she might have been. Precipitated by a life crisis, she went through a grieving response for that alter ego, and finally laid the ghost to rest through therapy. This grieving response can emerge at any time, but tends to happen when the person is finding life particularly challenging. It is, however, more usual in the child of seven or eight years old, as has already been discussed (see p. 22).

Other factors which influence individual responses

Not every parent responds to the birth of a baby with disfigurement in the same way, just as not every person reacts to disfigurement in the same way. This section focuses on some of the reasons for individuals reacting differently, on the ways in which individual responses influence the impact of disfigurement, and the meaning that it carries for the person with disfigurement.

Family reactions. When a baby is born with a visible disfigurement, parents nearly always go through a difficult and emotional period of adjustment. They have to let go of all they had anticipated and fantasized about their child and adjust to their less than perfect baby. This is described in more detail in Chapter 7 which looks at how you can best help in this situation. However, at this point it is worth illustrating how difficult this adjustment can be.

A little girl was born to parents who had longed for this child. When she was born, the father was the first to see her bilateral cleft lip. He wept, and took the child to his wife to see. She turned away with horror, and has a vivid memory of the 'ugly, ugly mess of a mouth'. She could not hold her baby for a few days, but was persuaded to look after her. She could not wait for surgery to repair the lip, and took no photos of her little girl until after that happened at three months. She said that 'Before the operation, she was a freak, and then she was normal and I could love her'. However, as her daughter grew up, she told her to explain to others that her lip was scarred because she had fallen on it. When I met the family, the child was 12 years old. The mother wept when she talked about the birth, and was still distressed. This mother had never got over the fact that she had given birth to a baby with a visible defect. She could not tolerate it or accept her child with a disfigurement. This may have been because she experienced it as an extension of her own feelings of inadequacy, and her self-esteem was so low that she could not live with this. She had used avoidance and denial as a way of living with it, and had encouraged her daughter to do the same, thus indicating to her that the cleft was intolerably shameful. However, this was not a good coping strategy for life, and the lack of acceptance of the disfigurement was still there under the surface.

Not all parents react in the same way and some find it easier to make the adjustment. Katy was the youngest of three children. She had a bilateral cleft lip and palate. When the parents saw her face, they were upset and shocked. However, after the first distress and concerns about Katy's future, they felt a sense of fierce protectiveness towards her. The mother said 'I felt like a leopardess with a cub: no one was going to come near her'. They wanted to take her home as quickly as possible, so that they could get used to it within their family. When she had her lip repaired, her mother said 'It's funny, I missed it, the way her lip curled over'.

The reasons why people respond as they do is not always easy to understand. It may be because of their own early experiences, when they felt that they were accepted and loved because of their appearance. This influences their own self-esteem, and their ability to tolerate any sense of failure, or of personal defect. Other family members often play a crucial role in helping parents accept their 'imperfect' child, and their reactions can explain a lot about the reaction of the parents. The following quotes illustrate two very different reactions from grandparents.

'Do you remember what your father said? He said, "If that's all that's wrong with her, she'll do for me."'

'My mother came to see us in the hospital. She said, "You've brought disgrace on the family."'

In our research, we found that the ability of grandparents to accept the child has a crucial effect on the parents' ability to adjust (Bradbury and Hewison, 1994a). Writers such as Fonagy *et al.* (1991) have described ways in which patterns of attachment can be carried down from generation to generation. Attachment theory describes the bonding process that happens when mother and baby interact and get to know each other. It is through the security of this attachment that the baby learns that he or she is accepted and loved unconditionally. Research has shown (Pastor, 1981) that babies who are insecurely attached to their mothers have greater difficulty forming social relationships when they are older. Main *et al.* (1985) found that mothers are more able to bond with their own babies when they themselves experienced good early attachment with their mothers.

Bettelheim (1972) described the importance of parental love and acceptance for the child.

Children can learn to live with a disability. But they cannot live well without the conviction that their parents find them utterly loveable ... If the parents, knowing his defect, love him now, he can believe that others will love him in the future. With this conviction he can live well now and have faith in the years to come.

Social support. The support of friends and neighbours can act as a buffer which helps a person to cope. This is true for parents when their child has a visible disfigurement, especially if this involves practical problems like hospital visits and help with other children. It is also important for a person to feel accepted by those around them, and close relationships with friends give a sense of social acceptance. In one study, Benson *et al.* (1991) found that mothers of babies with craniofacial conditions received less social support, and were less happy with the support they did receive, than other mothers. In our research (Bradbury and Hewison, 1994a), we found that those parents who found it difficult to adjust to their baby were more likely to find that friends and neighbours were less helpful than those of parents who adjusted well. However, studies have found that there may be a discrepancy between the objective amount of support and the individual's ability to utilize that support (Crockenberg, 1981); it is not the availability of the support which is as important as the individual's appraisal of it.

Personal qualities (resilience). It seems that a person's life experience will influence how they respond. However, it is also known that different people experiencing the same life events can respond in different ways. There has been a lot of interest in the concept of resilience and vulnerability in recent years, and researchers in this field have looked at those factors which help individuals cope with adversity. They have found that there are some individuals who have personal qualities which make them more able to withstand life's adversities; they seem to possess a 'self-righting' quality which enables them to bounce back from whatever happens to them. Some of the qualities of personality which have been identified as helping people cope include *intelligence, problem-solving skills, optimism, a sense of humour, acceptance by their parents* and *lack of early separations* (Fonagy *et al.*, 1994).

Gio was a bright little lad with a cheeky face and a marked nasal disfigurement. He had a particularly wicked sense of humour, and loved playing practical jokes. He went through a difficult time in his early teens, when he became more aware of the stares of others. However, he solved the problem by finding that if he winked at those who stared at him, they were taken aback and he was in control. He told me this with a broad grin on his face. Gio was part of a warm and caring family who shared his sense of humour. He also had the ability to problem-solve difficulties, and this gave him a deep sense of confidence which carried him through adversity. Thus his temperament, combined with a supportive and loving upbringing, gave him the strength to cope.

The Process Model of Stress and Coping

At this point it is useful to draw together all these factors in order to see how they interact in the process of coping with disfigurement. All those who have experienced visible disfigurement, either in themselves or in someone close to them, are faced with the need to cope with the situation. An influential coping model, developed by Lazarus and his associates (Lazarus, 1966), will be used to explain this process in the context of disfigurement. (The model has been slightly modified to allow for the particular experience of disfigurement.)

Lazarus has described coping as '*the process of managing demands (external or internal) that are appraised as taxing or exceeding the resources of the person*'. In other words, he saw coping as the ability to match stress with a person's resources to cope with that stress. Two people facing the same degree of pressure are likely to differ in their ability to cope with that stress, depending on resources such as qualities of temperament, family and social support and their past experience of dealing with other problems. Thus two people with the same disfigurement may cope with it in different ways.

Lazarus describes four components of coping.

- *Coping is an interactive **process**, not a single event.* It is an interaction between external and internal demands, and the handling of those demands. This process takes time and often runs a fluctuating course. At times it may seem as though everything is back to 'square one'. However, when someone is managing to cope, it is accompanied by an increasing sense of optimism and of gaining control over the situation.

  Mary has struggled to deal with the stares of strangers following a disfiguring injury (*external threat*). She is able to cope with the situation by talking it through with her husband and her friends. They encourage her to use her ability to think things through. Thus she is able to use her social resources (her friends and family) and her personal resources (her problem-solving capacity) to deal with difficulties as they arise.

- *Coping is viewed in terms of **management**, not mastery, which may not be possible.* Coping is seen by Lazarus as a dynamic process with the aim of *handling* the situation rather than resolving it. For those with disfigurement, external social pressures and internal feelings of difference make it difficult to arrive at a point when the problem has been solved – there are always new situations which will bring further stress. The process of coping is not a linear one, with a beginning and end, but moves from re-appraisal back to new issues relating to the experience of disfigurement. By successfully coping with one issue, the individual can become more confident and apply what has been learned to the next problem that comes along.

Simon badly injured his hand and it was very disfigured. At first he could not look at it himself but gradually learned to tolerate its appearance. He then found he was more able to cope with the feelings of self-consciousness when strangers saw it and stared at it. As he became more confident in public, he was more able to cope with the negative reactions to his hand by his small son.

- *Coping involves **appraisal**, and thus depends on the subjective evaluation of the individual.* By this, Lazarus suggests that appraisal of what is happening is central to the process of coping, and that appraisal is a subjective process. An individual's behaviour will be influenced by the sense that person makes of it, rather than by the judgement of someone else.

Jennifer was born with a facial disfigurement. As she grew up, her parents helped her to understand why people stared at her and what she could do about it. Her appraisal of the situation was that she was loved for herself, and that other people's reactions were their problems, not hers. She had to re-evaluate this when she started going out with a boy who seemed loving at first and then laughed about her clinging behaviour to his friends. She felt foolish and ashamed of her behaviour, but then coped by realizing that she behaved that way because of her insecurity about her appearance.

- *Coping is a **mobilization of effort**, both cognitive and behavioural.* In order to cope, the individual needs to gather his or her resources, and deal with the situation by thinking about it and then by doing things to improve matters. Thinking alone is not enough; it does not change the objective reality of the problems faced by those with disfigurement. Behavioural changes alone are not enough to successfully cope if there is no change in the person's understanding of what is happening.

Peter has facial disfigurement following treatment for cancer. He has coped with his altered perceptions of himself and the world around him by thinking hard about how he will deal with the changes in his life, and then by working hard at explaining things to those who ask and ignoring those who stare. It takes a lot of effort on his part, and he does have to constantly think about whether he is successful in what he is doing. The experience has taught him a lot about himself and about others and he feels stronger as an individual because of this.

Lazarus' model is a useful one in that it provides a framework for drawing together the various factors which influence the process of coping with disfigurement.

SUMMARY

❑ There are common psychological and social problems experienced by those with disfigurement. These include:
1. difficulties in social encounters
2. disruption to normal patterns of work and play
3. disruption to the body image
4. coping with treatment and making decisions about treatment
5. post-traumatic stress
6. parental adjustment to the birth
7. the responses of family and friends
8. coping with the media

❑ These are influenced by:
1. historical attitudes towards congenital disfigurement ('the wrath of the gods')
2. cultural perceptions of attractiveness ('what is beautiful is good')
3. stigmatizing social reactions to the visibly different

❑ However, not everyone reacts in the same way to these problems. Factors which mediate individual responses include:
1. age: the impact of disfigurement at different ages
2. the type of disfigurement: a) its severity
                                              b) its location on the body
                                              c) the meaning that it has for the individual
                                              d) whether it is congenital or traumatic
3. Other factors include: a) family reactions
                                     b) social support
                                     c) personal resilience

❑ A process model of stress and coping was described to give an understanding of the coping process. In this model, coping is seen as:
a) an interactive process rather than a single event
b) management rather than mastery
c) appraisal and subjective evaluation
d) mobilization of effort and resources

3

The Helping Process

In the last chapter, we looked at the type of problems which can confront those with a visible disfigurement. They face common problems which have their roots in psychological, social and historical processes, but we have also seen that there are factors within the individual, and within the social world of the individual, which mediate these problems and help the person to cope. Every individual is unique, and there is no doubt that there are many people with visible disfigurement who cope well and do not need help beyond their resources of self, family and friends.

However, those who work in the field of disfigurement know that not everyone copes with the problems, and indeed some people experience great difficulties. The purpose of this chapter is to consider how best this help can be offered to those who need it within the context of a general helping process. Before going on to specific forms of help for those with disfigurement, it is worthwhile pausing to consider what we are trying to do when we set out to help and how we can shape the process of helping in order to make it an effective process.

General Principles of the Helping Process

The general principles underlying the helping process are best expressed in contrast with their opposites.

- **facilitation** v. **prescription:** *facilitating the process of coping and adjustment rather than prescribing what should be done.* The helping process is intended to encourage the individual to find ways of coping, not to tell that person how to cope. It is very tempting to look at the problem and suggest what can be done, especially if that seems to be what everyone wants. However, only the individual fully understands his or her own strengths and weaknesses and only the individual can truly appraise his or her own resources. We cannot be experts on the individual; people are experts on themselves and all we can do is facilitate their own expertise. By doing so, we encourage the individual to become self-sufficient and to gain a sense of competence.

- **normalization** v. **professionalization:** *working towards normal social and family environments and networks rather than dependence on professionals.* In Chapter 1, I described the professionals who are likely to become involved in the life of the individual with disfigurement. The temptation is to minimize the ability of the individual to cope without this professional help, and to maximize potential social problems. This can disrupt normal patterns of social support and social functioning, leaving the individual dependent on professionals and isolated from normal networks.

- **equality** v. **dominance:** *working together as equal partners, sharing expertise rather than dominating the situation as a professional.* Someone in need of help can feel emotionally vulnerable. When the helping process is effectively engaged, the helper encourages the person to build strengths and to feel a true sense of equality in that helping relationship. If the helper is using professional experience and knowledge to dominate and control the process, then the person being helped is being encouraged to remain weak and vulnerable.

- **empowerment** v. **control:** *encouraging the person to use their own expertise and skills to take control rather than the professional keeping control.* An important element of helping is empowerment. The helper can encourage the individual to work through difficulties, to seek solutions and to gain mastery. This process will be impeded if the helper takes over the situation and substitutes *professional* skills for individual skills. Thus the helper should strive to build up the individual's confidence in his or her own ability to handle the situation, even though that may not be the quickest way of resolving the situation.

- **change** v. **stasis:** *helping to bring about change rather than becoming stuck in the same situation.* This is a very important principle of the helping process which can get lost in day-to-day work. There is no point in helping if there is no outcome in terms of change. Emotional support can be effective if it helps someone cope with difficulties, but it serves no purpose within a helping framework if it maintains the situation and does not actually help anyone, except possibly the helper to feel wanted!

These are the general principles of the helping process. It is important to refer back to them from time to time in order to appraise what is happening within the helping relationship.

The Structure of the Helping Process

Based on these important underlying principles, the helping process can be described within the following framework:

1. establishing the relationship
2. identifying the problems and resources
3. setting the aims
4. working together to achieve those aims
5. evaluating outcome
6. drawing the process to a conclusion

The process needs to be flexible. If there is no change, then it is necessary to look again at the individual's problems and resources in the light of what has happened, and re-define the aims. Our perceptions of problems and resources may be biased or limited, becoming more clear once the helping process is underway.

Establishing the relationship

A helping relationship should be a dynamic interactive process, during which both people involved come to feel a sense of mutual trust and acceptance. In order to establish such a relationship, there are issues that need to be addressed.

Recruiting the individual. As was discussed in Chapter 2, those with physical problems may be reluctant to talk about their emotional problems. They may feel a sense of personal failure because of problems they are having in coping with the situation; they may also believe that others see them as suffering some sort of mental breakdown. Both these beliefs can cause the individual to feel threatened and can reinforce feelings of defensiveness based on an awareness of being visibly different from others. Thus it is particularly important for the helper to avoid assuming a mental health role, but to work towards a relationship which treats this process as a normal part of the person's general care.

Michael had injured his hand in an industrial accident, and was referred to the counsellor by the surgeon who observed that he was keeping his hand hidden away. He came to see the counsellor feeling very defensive, and was angry that the surgeon had made the referral. Michael was someone who had always coped with problems, and had laughed at people who saw a 'shrink'. The counsellor explained that what he had to deal with was an unusual experience. She suggested that whilst he was clearly someone used to dealing with things, the accident to his hand had created a particular set of problems for him which he had not met before. Her role was to help him deal with these problems by applying his coping skills to this unusual situation. Thus she encouraged his belief in his own ability to cope, whilst suggesting that the current situation was unusual, and related to a specific event. She emphasized his role in the process, which allowed him to relax, and feel more comfortable and less threatened. The prerequisite for establishing this relationship was for the counsellor to explore the negative feelings he brought to the counselling situation.

This approach applies to whoever is involved as the helper, whether it is the psychologist, the surgeon, the nurse on the ward or anyone else who is available and willing to help. The principle remains the same; it is important to **normalize** the individual's experience and to encourage the belief that he or she is responding in an understandable way to a difficult situation, and that any help that is offered is based on mutual effort.

Agreeing a contract. It is important that both the helper and the individual are clear about their commitment to the helping relationship, and that the commitment should be clearly defined. This is known as a **contract**. It requires both parties to agree about the presenting problems, the aims of the intervention, the length and location of each session, the intervals between sessions and when progress and outcome will be evaluated.

Janine had a baby with a cleft lip and palate. She was a single parent with two other children, struggling to cope with financial problems, and having problems feeding the baby. She was also worried about getting to hospital for appointments and managing hospital admissions. She had adjusted to her baby's appearance and was not too worried about that. The health visitor called to see her and they agreed a contract: the health visitor would call twice a week until feeding was well-established and Janine felt confident in handling her child. At the same time, she would put Janine in touch with social services to arrange financial and practical help for hospital visits and the care of her other children. At the end of each week they would decide whether the health visitor needed to visit during the following week. The intervention was specific and focused on the presenting problems, and both Janine and the health visitor were clear about their commitment to the helping process.

It may be that other problems emerge during this period of help, such as coping with the reactions of others to the baby's appearance. In this situation, Janine and the health visitor would decide whether they wanted to work together on this problem, whether this would alter the intervals between the home visits and when they would evaluate progress and outcome. When the helper is visiting at home, and when there are other problems in the family situation, it is all too easy to get drawn into an unproductive long-term relationship which is unsatisfactory to both the helper and the individual. A clear contract helps to shape the boundaries within which the helping relationship can flourish and be most effective. A helping relationship generally takes time to develop, but it is an essential part of the whole helping process, and needs to be established before any effective help can be offered. The principles of this relationship should underpin the care which is offered to the individual by all the professionals involved.

Identifying the Problems and Resources

In order to identify the problems faced by the person with disfigurement and the resources that may help them to cope, the helper needs to be able to listen effectively and to encourage the individual to examine problems and resources in an open way. There are both verbal and non-verbal ways of facilitating this.

Verbal communication

• *Asking questions.* The helper will generally need to direct early encounters by asking questions in such a way as to gain information and to focus on the issues. There are three broad types of questions: *open-ended, close-ended* and *rhetorical* questions.

  Open-ended questions, such as, 'And how did that make you feel?', allows the person to respond freely. It makes no assumptions about what the answer should be, and therefore is useful as a way of encouraging the individual to talk in an open way. This type of question facilitates communication and helps the gathering of information about the person's emotional state.

  A close-ended question, for example, 'When did you start to worry about this?', requires factual responses and may be useful when more specific information is required. However, it does not encourage the person to expand on what is said and the information gained will be limited.

A rhetorical question, such as, 'That must have been awful for you, mustn't it?', is of very little value in facilitating communication and gathering information. It assumes what the answer will be, and is only asked in order to gain confirmation of that answer. Thus it makes the person asking the question feel powerful and in control of the situation, whilst making the person on the receiving end feel helpless. For someone who is unsure about what he or she is feeling, the rhetorical question can shape reactions and manipulate feelings. Rhetorical questions should always be avoided in the helping relationship.

*   *Focusing the discussion (reflecting back).* The helper can help the listening process by reflecting back on what has been said in order to clarify it. This can be done by repeating something of significance that has been said and probing it further. For example, if the individual says that he or she now tends to stay at home and is worried about social situations, then this needs to be understood in terms of identifying problems. The helper could say, 'You are worried about going out socially – tell me about that'.
*   *Summarizing.* It is useful to summarize the discussion at the end of each session by drawing out the main points and identifying the problems and resources which have been raised. This encourages the individual to feel that someone has listened to them and that he or she has been heard. It also clarifies the issues for both individuals. It is sometimes helpful to write the points of the summary down.

Non-verbal communication

*   *Positioning.* It is best to sit in a quiet and private place with comfortable chairs, where you will not be disturbed. The chairs should be placed at an angle and not opposite each other or with a desk between. Sitting directly face to face can be very challenging and makes it difficult for the individual to look away when he or she needs to think. A desk between the chairs forms a tangible barrier which affects communication by establishing a power relationship – the person behind the desk is clearly in charge! The chairs should be close enough for both to feel comfortable, but not close enough to be seen as an invasion of space. The chairs should be roughly equal in height so that good eye contact can be maintained and one person does not feel dominant over the other.
*   *Eye contact.* When someone is talking to another person they often look away to gather their thoughts. The listener needs to maintain eye contact whilst the person is talking so that when the individual

looks back, he or she knows the other person has been listening. Notes should not be made during the session as this can impede the listening process; they should be made immediately after the session is finished. If the helper feels it is important to make notes during the session, permission should be sought from the individual, and some explanation given as to why (e.g. 'It would help me to write down some of the information you are giving me so that I don't forget it afterwards – is that O.K. with you?').

• *Posture and facial expression.* Other forms of non-verbal communication are also important as we often communicate with each other by non-verbal signals. The helper should try to sit in an open, non-defensive posture with arms uncrossed and relaxed. Responding to what is being said with appropriate facial expressions is particularly important. The individual will look at the helper's face and if the helper looks bored or upset, then that will influence the encounter. Clothes can be important – there are times when it is reasonable to take off the white coat and move out of that particular professional role. Clothes that are too casual or dirty imply a lack of respect for the individual; clothes that are too smart may make the individual feel uncomfortable. What we wear has an impact on others, and thought should be given to this issue.

Whatever means may be used to understand the problems faced by the person with disfigurement and to identify their resources, they are most effective and meaningful when carried out within the context of the helping relationship. Once the problems and resources have been identified, the next step is to set aims and objectives.

The Structure of the Individual Session

The helping process is made up of a series of individual sessions, the number of which will have been decided when the contract was agreed, and then modified as necessary following further evaluation and re-appraisal. It is important to give some consideration to the structure of the individual session.

Patrick was a very talkative young man who had suffered burns to his hands. He was very upset about this and wanted to talk about it. He took over the session and talked at length about all his problems, getting more and more agitated. At the end of the hour the helper had to leave and thus had to break into the flow of talk and end the session. Patrick was left feeling upset as he walked out the door.

The helper had made no attempt to structure the session and Patrick was not helped but went away feeling upset. The general structure of each session could be as follows:

- *Introduction:* there should be an introductory period in which general comments are made to relax both people and to settle into the session. Comments about that British obsession, the weather, are useful as a sort of elaborate verbal greeting.
- *Summarizing and anticipation:* After the greeting, the helper should summarize what has been said and done before, and they should both then discuss what was to be dealt with in this session.
- *The main part of the session:* Most of the session (between 30 minutes and 45 minutes of a 60-minute session) should be given over to the main work of the session. There should be enough time for the person to express emotion and for the process of helping to take place.
- *Drawing the session to a close:* The main part of the session may be very intense, and the helper should recognize the importance of reducing the emotional level of the session towards its end. The last part of the session (about 10 minutes) should be a 'cooling-down' period in which the helper encourages the individual to calm down and talk in a lighter way, summarizing what has been said and framing the next step.
- *Farewells:* The individual can then leave with some light farewell comments and an agreement about the time and place of the next session.

Potential difficulties in maintaining this structure

- *Keeping to time:* It is important not to lose track of the time, but looking at a watch is a powerful gesture which may signal boredom. The issue of time should be clearly discussed, and having a time-piece clearly visible to both is useful.
- *The 'doorstep revelation':* a common phenomenon is the 'doorstep revelation' when the individual blurts out something of great importance just as he or she is leaving. This should be acknowledged, with the clearly-stated understanding that it will be dealt with at the next session.
- *Wasting time:* sometimes too much time is spent on greetings and general chat. This is particularly likely to happen when two people know each other well, having worked together for some time, or when either finds it hard to deal with the real difficulties, and so uses

general chat as a way of avoiding the actual problems. The helper should be disciplined and restrict such talk to a warm and friendly greeting and introduction.

Thus the structure of individual sessions reflects the overall structure of the helping process, having a beginning, a middle and an end. A sense of structure provides a framework within which the work of effective helping can take place.

Setting the Aims

It is now time to work together to set the aims of the helping process. These aims will help to identify what change needs to take place and to evaluate whether that change has occurred at the end of the helping process. There are three main considerations to take into account in this process.

1. **Are the aims long-term, medium-term or short-term?** Long-term aims, such as finding peace of mind, or adjusting to the disfigurement, tend to be fairly general and take time to achieve. They may never be achieved *within* the time-span of the helping process but may eventually be achieved *as a result of* that process. Medium and short-term aims, such as getting back to school or re-establishing former relationships tend to be more specific and more focused, and can be achieved over a shorter time span. Short-term aims, such as making contact with school to ensure that work is set while in hospital are generally used as a means of achieving the other longer-term aims. It is not always easy to set long-term aims, particularly at times of crisis when everything is confused and unclear. At such times, short-term and limited aims can be a useful way of directing energies. Longer-term aims will become more clear as time goes by, but should not be ignored. The helper should ensure that the long-term aims are not lost and are clear to all those involved.

2. **Are the aims realistic?** The development of realistic aims is essential to the helping process, and depends on a clear understanding of the person's personal and social resources, and of the problems to be faced. Unrealistic aims can have consequences that are harmful. For example, it would be unrealistic for someone with a severely disfigured face to aim to walk down the street without being stared at, whilst it *would* be realistic to aim to cope with the stares of others. In terms of the process model of coping, the aim would be to achieve mastery rather than to resolve the problem. Unrealistic aims discourage change, as it becomes apparent to all that they are not

possible, and thus there is no way of directing the helping process. They may build an inevitable failure into the situation, thus increasing the person's sense of worthlessness and low self-esteem.

3. **Whose aims are they?** Those who set the aims should be those who will be involved in the helping process. The individual concerned is clearly the central person, but it may well be appropriate also to work with the parents of a young child, as a way of helping them to help the child. The age at which the child is competent to be involved is a matter of judgement on the part of the parents and the helper. Difficulties may arise when there is a conflict between the needs of the parents and the needs of the child. It may be that the parents feel guilty about the disfigurement and want the child to have surgery to help them feel less guilty; they feel as if they are doing something. However, the child may be untroubled about the disfigurement and may not wish to go through surgery.

General aims to help people with disfigurement

General problems associated with disfigurement have been described in Chapter 2. Individual reactions and styles of coping can vary, and the importance of recognizing individual responses has already been discussed. However, there are general aims which relate to this area of work, and these general aims can guide and inform the establishment of *individual* aims. These aims are:

- *Exploration and resolution of emotions, thoughts and feelings regarding the disfigurement, treatment, other people's responses etc.;*
- *Empowerment through the development of coping strategies to deal with social responses;*
- *Working towards effective and realistic cognitive appraisal of the responses of others;*
- *Integration and acceptance of body image;*
- *Facilitation of effective decision-making regarding treatment;*
- *Restoration of normal patterns of family and social support.*

Working together to achieve the aims

Once the problems and resources have been identified and the aims have been set, the time has come to bring about change by finding ways of achieving these aims. There are many ways in which change can be brought about by the helping process, and these will be discussed in more detail in the next few chapters.

Evaluating outcome

The evaluation of outcome is integral to the helping process, and should happen as the helping process proceeds, rather than being left until the end. Regular evaluation ensures that both the individual and the helper remain clear about what they are doing and why they are doing it. It also encourages a flexible approach in which the help can be modified if it is not working, or if new problems arise. This is the secondary appraisal of coping described in Lazarus' model.

It may be that aims are met quite rapidly, and both individual and helper feel that the helping process can now be drawn to a conclusion. However, it could also be that not all of the aims have been met. In that case, the helper and the individual need to consider what has been achieved and whether that was enough, or whether they want to look again at the problems and resources and modify the aims accordingly. This allows the process to remain flexible and responsive to individual needs.

The helper may benefit from evaluating progress both with the individual and with a supervisor who can oversee the process in a more detached way. The issue of supervision is discussed in Chapter 8.

Drawing the helping process to a conclusion

There comes a point in the helping process when it is reasonable to draw things to a conclusion. An important principle of helping is to move from *professionalization* to *normalization*. It can be very tempting to prolong the process unduly and to build up the individual's dependency on the helper, particularly when the problems are complex and there seem to be few external resources. The individual is then at risk of becoming enmeshed in a professional environment, unable to gain mastery and control, and thus unable to cope effectively with life.

The conclusion of the helping process should be planned and reached by mutual agreement. Sometimes it ends abruptly because the individual finds it unhelpful and fails to turn up again. It may also be that the helper finds it difficult to discuss conclusions with the individual and allows the helping process to drift into an unsatisfactory ending where the individual fails to keep appointments. If the helping process has been effective and useful, then its conclusion becomes a constructive part of that process. Concluding the process allows both the individual and the helper to recognize what has been achieved and to identify ways in which that can be generalized to future situations.

William suffered burns to his hands and face and has been seeing the liaison nurse from the burns unit since discharge from the hospital. Together they have explored the new problems he is facing and the resources he has to deal with them. They have tried different ways of coping with these until William began to feel more positive and more in control. He discussed this with the nurse and said that he now feels that he has more confidence and has learnt some useful strategies for dealing with his anger and his social problems. The nurse has encouraged his confidence and emphasized the courage it had taken and the way he had recovered from difficulties and had coped. They have agreed that she does not need to see him again, and both see this as a very positive step. The helping process is now complete.

However, the conclusion of the helping process can be difficult for both the helper and the individual. Working together at times of trauma and need can create a bond between the two which may be difficult to break, so the conclusion should not be abrupt but should be planned and reached as a joint activity. If the individual has become too dependent on the helper, then he or she may feel abandoned and rejected. Equally, the helper may feel a sense of loss. The ending of the helping process should be seen as part of that process, and should be linked to the initial contract, the setting of aims and the appraisal of outcome. Offering to be available for further contact smoothes the transition and helps the individual to feel that he or she has not been abandoned and that there is a point of contact that can be used in the future if any further difficulties arise. In practice, people rarely take up this offer, but generally say that they feel better knowing that help is available if they do need it. If the helping process has been effective, then the ending becomes a positive step towards the normalization of the individual's life. Thus the underlying principle of *normalization* rather than *professionalization* will shape the transition from helping process to coping without help.

SUMMARY

❏ General principles of the helping process which characterize and shape this process:
1. facilitation rather than prescription
2. normalization rather than professionalization
3. equality rather than dominance
4. empowerment rather than control
5. change rather than stasis

❏ The helping process has a framework and passes through a series of stages:
1. establishing the relationship – enlisting the individual
                                   – agreeing a contract
2. identifying problems and resources – verbal and non-verbal communication
3. setting aims – are they long-term or short term, are they realistic, and whose aims are they?
4. working together to achieve those aims
5. evaluating outcome
6. drawing the process to a conclusion

❏ The general pattern of this framework is mirrored in each individual session:
1. introduction
2. summarizing and anticipation
3. the main part of the session
4. drawing to a close
5. farewells

❏ There are potential difficulties in maintaining this structure, and these include:
1. keeping to time and ensuring that each stage of the session has enough time
2. 'doorstep' revelations as the person is leaving
3. wasting time by too much general discussion

Helping People with Disfigurement: the Qualities of a Skilled Helper

The last chapter dealt with the structure of the helping process. In this chapter, we will look at the individual qualities which make a good helper and ways in which the helper can develop his or her skills. Many of these qualities are general counselling skills, but there are some factors related to the issue of disfigurement which are specific to this field.

The Qualities of a Skilled Helper

What are the qualities of a good helper? A useful source of reference for this can be found in the writings of Rogers (for example, 1959). He was a pioneer in the field of counselling and remains an important authority whose work has influenced many counsellors and psychologists. He understood that for the helping process to be effective, the helper utilizes his or her own personal qualities as part of that process. These personal qualities include the following:

Personal warmth. Rogers considered this to be a fundamental quality of the skilled helper. It can be expressed to the individual by the way in which the helper responds to his or her feelings and concerns. It requires the helper to become involved in the client's needs in a caring way; this can be expressed to the individual with a warm smile, responding in a warm and caring way to the individual and showing an interest in that person's life beyond the presenting problem. Noticing that the young boy has new trainers, or laughing with the individual about something in the news all help to show warmth and regard for that person's individuality. The warmth felt by the counsellor for the client encourages the client to feel esteemed, and to feel safe. It can help to touch the person on the arm or hold the person's hand when they are upset, but this should always be done with sensitive awareness of how it may be received. For some people, touch in this context may be perceived as intrusive and controlling, causing them to set up defensive barriers. To others, it may signal sensitivity and caring.

Self-esteem. To do the helping work effectively, the helper should have good self-esteem. This does not mean feeling self-satisfied, but does require a fundamental sense of self-worth and an ability to tolerate criticism. It is the helper's self-esteem which gives strength and resilience, and this will be conveyed to the individual. Those who have good self-esteem will have a realistic and optimistic sense of their own worth and will be able to draw on their own resources to validate this. The helper with good self-esteem can tolerate anger and distress on the part of the individual without taking it personally and becoming defensive or rejecting.

Spontaneity. The effective helper has the personal ability to show spontaneity and be flexible in his or her thinking and behaviour within the helping relationship. This becomes apparent when the individual suddenly changes in mood or behaviour or when the helper gets lost in the process of trying to help. A spontaneous and flexible response is to acknowledge what is happening and to be open to change and to new ideas. Those lacking in this quality become fixed on their own assessment and find it difficult to react appropriately to what is actually happening.

Genuineness. The helper who has this personal quality is genuine in his or her desire to help and is not using the situation to manipulate or control. There are no hidden agendas, and the individual feels safe to respond in an open way and to take risks, knowing that the helper is a safe person to talk to. The helper does not distort what is being said in order to fit this into his or her own framework. The individual responds to a genuine helper with trust, and the helper with this quality will also trust the individual.

Unconditional positive regard. Rogers describes this quality as being of fundamental importance. It involves respect for the other person and a belief that the individual's experiences and beliefs are important. The helper is able to accept the individual without criticism or judgement. This quality is demonstrated by the way in which the helper listens, responding to what is being said in an accepting way without criticism. The individual may have carried out some action which makes the helper critical, such as being involved in a violent fight. The individual may also live a life-style which is very different to that of the helper, such as being a transsexual. It is important for the helper to put aside any sense of criticism or moral judgement. If this is impossible, then it is better to find someone else to do the work.

Empathy. Rogers described this quality as being willing to attempt to understand the individual. The helper who is empathic is open to the beliefs, hopes and the daily life experience of the individual. Whilst it may not always be possible to fully understand another's world view and inner life, the empathic helper attempts to do so and thus responds within the context of the individual. Empathy is a very different response to sympathy. When someone feels sympathy, then he or she feels pity. This can be a demoralizing reaction for someone struggling to cope with adversity. A sympathetic approach may be kindly in intent, but places a distance between the helper and the individual and puts the helper on a higher moral plane. An empathic response allows the helper to express a sense of solidarity and mutual understanding based on a common humanity. The emotions expressed by the individual are understood and accepted at an emotional level by the helper.

Non-defensiveness This quality is part of what has already been described above and is only included for emphasis at this point. The helper should be able to examine his or her own responses and should not allow them to get in the way of the helping process. If the helper strives to develop the qualities described above, then he or she will be open to the needs of the other person and not put up barriers between them as a means of self-protection. There may be factors which cause the relationship to be characterized by defensiveness on the side of the helper, the individual or on both sides. The importance of self-esteem by the helper has been discussed. A person lacking in self-esteem is more likely to be closed and defended, and thus less able to hear all that is said and respond effectively. This issue is of great importance when working in the field of disfigurement, when the person with a visible difference may feel defensive and the helper may have problems coping with his or her own reactions to the disfigurement.

These personal qualities are fundamental in the helping process. Anyone who finds themselves in a helping role within this context should understand the way in which their personal qualities will profoundly influence the helping process. Although there are many ways in which help can be structured, the quality of the relationship which is formed between the helper and the individual is the foundation upon which all else is based. Thus personal qualities are reflected in the helping relationship.

The Helping Relationship

The qualities of the skilled helper are personal to that helper, but as the helping process is engaged, they will be reflected in that process. When the helper shows these personal qualities, then the relationship with the individual seeking help is characterized by the following:

Equality: that both parties feel they are equal partners in the relationship. When the relationship is unequal, then one party is exercising control over the other. The controlling person may be the helper, using professional status or a sense of greater personal efficacy. It could also be the individual being helped, who may control the relationship using superior social status, dominance and anger or defensiveness. The person in control may be kindly and benevolent, but such inequality restricts and disempowers the other person. Issues of equality may arise when the individual being helped has learning difficulties, is very young or very old, or when the person's normal coping skills and sense of personal authority has been undermined by trauma and/or illness. In such cases, special care should be taken to ensure that as much equality as possible underpins the interaction.

Open communication: that there is free and open communication within the helping relationship. Ways in which this can be facilitated have been described in Chapter 3. There can only be such open communication when there is mutual trust and respect, and when both partners strive together to pool their resources in order to understand the situation and to bring about change. This type of communication is a two-way process with information and expertise flowing in both directions.

Negotiation: that the relationship is flexible and open to change. Aims and expectations may need to be altered as time goes by. The contract which sets a framework of time and place may be modified. If there is equality between partners, then this negotiation is an important way in which the relationship can develop. However, if the helper is dominating the relationship, then negotiation is supplanted by manipulation and control.

Qualities of Skilled Helping in the Field of Visible Disfigurement

The qualities both of the individual and of the relationship described in the preceding paragraph have a particular relevance to the field of disfigurement, where the reactions of both the helper and the individual to the disfigurement can be intense. The following factors can cause problems for those carrying out this work.

Losing sight of the individual behind the disfigurement

As I have already discussed, there are common problems facing those with visible disfigurement, but every individual has their own unique responses and their own resources. Because the visual impact of the disfigurement can be very powerful, the person behind the disfigurement may get lost.

Peter went to see his GP, feeling depressed. He had undergone radical surgery to his face following the removal of a tumour. His face was distorted by this, and at first the GP felt that this stopped him going out. By allowing him to talk things through in an open way, the GP understood that Peter had accepted his face, but was depressed because he was unemployed and had financial problems. It was lack of money, and shame about his reduced status, which kept him inside.

The GP's first response was very understandable; Peter had an obvious facial disfigurement and was depressed and socially isolated, and therefore it seemed logical to assume that he must be disturbed about the disfigurement. By establishing a relationship which allowed Peter to talk through his concerns, the GP was able to make a more accurate assessment of the problems and therefore offer the most appropriate help.

It is particularly important to take time to assess the situation, even when the helper identifies closely with the individual or they share similar backgrounds. This is also true, however, when the backgrounds are very different, and beliefs about class, culture and ethnic groups prejudice the helper's thinking. We are all prone to jump to conclusions, but a good and accurate assessment requires the helper to work from what the individual has to say rather than what the helper believes to be true. It is important to see the individual behind the stereotype. In order to move beyond the stereotype and identify problems and resources, the helper needs to be able to listen effectively. Skilled listening requires that the helper listens intently to what is said and picks out the important points. These are then reflected back to the person in order to ensure that the helper has got it right. When someone feels that they are being heard and understood, then they are encouraged to open up and talk more freely. The process of skilled listening also helps to focus attention on what is important for the helping process. The personal qualities of a skilled helper, reflected in the helping relationship, facilitate this process. Thus personal warmth, unconditional positive regard and non-defensiveness are all part of skilled listening.

The impact of the disfigurement on the helper

An issue which arises time and again for those working with people with disfigurement is that of their own response. The helper is not immune to cultural and social responses, nor to feelings of distress or aversion, as the following illustrates.

A seriously burnt little girl was brought in to the unit. She had full thickness burns to her face, and would be severely disfigured. The surgeon operating on her had a daughter the same age. He said, 'If that was my daughter, I would kill her and then kill myself.'

This young surgeon had been shaken and upset. His feelings needed to be acknowledged, and he needed support at this time. Soon he would have to talk to the girl's family, and it was likely that he would be treating her for some time. He felt her situation was hopeless, and this sense of despair could dominate his approach to the family and the child. He had seen burns before, but it was the fact that he identified the child with his daughter that caused the emotional impact. This surgeon had been trained to treat such cases; those who are not used to disfigurement may be even more shocked at what they see.

Their initial response may almost be as if the person is experiencing the disfigurement as if it were their own, or as if it had happened to someone who feels part of them, like their own child. This can cause people to feel threatened and defensive, as they strive subconsciously to reject this feeling in order to protect themselves. Because they may feel guilty about their responses, they may suppress their feelings, which can have an insidious effect on the helping relationship.

Some forms of disfigurement may be very shocking at first sight, and the following guidelines may be useful when meeting the person for the first time.

- *Where possible, find photos of similar types of disfigurement before seeing the person, in order to prepare yourself, so that the initial response is not one of shock.*

- *Spend a little time in your initial encounter discussing the disfigurement. This allows you to focus on it, to get the details of it clear, and then allows the focus to shift from it. It will also allow the person to show you the disfigurement and thus remain in control of the situation.*
- *Talk through your feelings with someone else, either a colleague or supervisor.*

The helper may be seen by the family or the person with disfigurement as representative of social responses, so a calm response which acknowledges the disfigurement without distress can be of great benefit. The helper should not be ashamed of his or her feelings, but should acknowledge them and examine them *away* from the helping situation. This can be facilitated by working with another professional who acts as supervisor. The issue of supervision will be discussed further in Chapter 8.

Feelings of loss of competence

When confronted by a terrible and devastating injury, such as major burns or loss of limbs, then the helper may feel that he or she has neither the competence nor the experience to deal with it. This feeling of helplessness can be conveyed to the individual with the injury and to their family, making the problem seem overwhelming.

Wayne was a 17-year-old boy who contracted mengicoccal meningitis. He was taken to hospital and lapsed into unconsciousness. Whilst he was unconscious, he developed gangrene in all four limbs and had surgery to remove both legs above the knee, and both hands. The staff at the intensive care unit did not know what to say to him when he eventually came round. They panicked as they felt this was too horrific to cope with, and felt that if it was their son, or themselves, they would not have wanted to live. They felt incompetent to deal with this as they had never come across this problem in such a young boy before.

The nursing staff were very stressed by this situation and felt unable to help. A liaison psychiatrist met with them to help them identify what there was in this situation which they had met before, such as working with people with spinal cord injuries. He also encouraged the staff to recognize that Wayne's problems were not their problems, and that he was different from them and their sons, being a separate individual in his own right. This helped them to generalize their helping skills and to re-establish their ability to help. It also encouraged them to look at Wayne's individual needs and those of his family, thus shifting the focus from their emotional responses to the needs of the individual. When Wayne did come round, they were not overwhelmed and could offer him effective help.

The qualities of skilled helping are vital to the helping process. By being aware of these qualities and the impact that they have on the individual, the helper can try to develop those qualities and use them to greatest effect in offering help and bringing about change.

SUMMARY

❏ The skilled helper should show personal qualities in the relationship which will allow an effective relationship to develop. These include:
1. personal warmth
2. self-esteem
3. spontaneity
4. sincerity
5. unconditional positive regard
6. empathy
7. genuineness
8. non-defensiveness

❏ These qualities are reflected in the helping relationship, which is characterized by:
1. equality
2. open communication
3. negotiation

❏ In the field of disfigurement, there are potential problems which can influence the helper's responses to the individual with disfigurement:
1. losing sight of the person behind the disfigurement (stereotyping)
2. the impact of the disfigurement on the helper, giving rise to feelings of personal distress
3. feelings of loss of competence, when the situation seems too devastating.

5

Meeting the Needs: Establishing the Relationship

We have considered problems faced by those with disfigurement and how the helping process can work to bring about effective change. The principles underlying this process are based on good counselling practice which aims to empower the individual to cope with life's adversities, and this chapter examines how this process can be put into practice in the initial stages of working with people with disfigurement. Case studies taken from clinical work, with details changed to protect the anonymity of the people involved, will be used to illustrate this. Ways of helping will be described, and skills relevant to each stage of the process will be discussed.

When the Adult Needs to Talk: Coping with Emotions

People talking about their disfigurement can become very emotional, especially if they have hidden their feelings for many years because of shame or lack of support. Whilst it is tempting to jump in with reassurance and try to calm the person down, this can minimize the problem, making the individual feel that they should not be getting so upset. In establishing the relationship, it is important to listen effectively and to allow the person to express their feelings, however painful these may be.

Maria. When she was 30 years old Maria had an acoustic neuroma (tumour of the ear) removed from the right side of her head. At the time she was married and had two young children. She was left with a marked droop on the right side of her face. She became preoccupied by this, and felt extremely self-conscious about her appearance. Her facial expression was distorted by the palsy, and she felt that her smile was crooked. Everyone told her she was lucky to be alive, and she felt guilty about the way she felt, which increased her misery. She found social encounters very stressful, and began to find excuses to avoid mixing with others. Her husband grew increasingly impatient with her, and she became more and more preoccupied and withdrawn. Before the operation, she had been a fun-loving and outgoing person, but now she felt that she was losing any sense of herself, and becoming someone she did not recognize, either in the mirror, or in her own behaviour. Her confidence disappeared, and she felt lost and helpless. At the time, there was no one to whom she could talk and she felt abandoned by those who had treated her. She came to seek surgery 10 years after her operation, following an article she had seen in the paper. She was told by the surgeon that reconstructive surgery would improve her face to some extent, but not completely, and would leave her with scars. The need to make this decision brought up a lot of old issues, and had made her very anxious and upset. Because she had not adjusted to her face, she felt unable to decide what to do about changing it, and experienced a major identity and body image crisis. She described herself as a 'flower in bud' who had lost 10 years of her life and had never developed. This all came out when she talked with the liaison nurse who worked with the surgeon.

The initial encounter with Maria was highly emotional. She felt so ashamed and stigmatized by her appearance that she had never been able to speak about it, and spent most of the first session in tears. The nurse listened carefully, but said little apart from what was needed to say to encourage Maria to talk freely. She was warm in her greeting and her approach to Maria, smiling and showing an interest and an empathic concern. She sat with Maria and touched her arm from time to time when she got particularly upset, but did not attempt to stop her crying. When Maria apologized for crying, the nurse told her she was glad that she felt able to show her feelings, and made sure there were plenty of tissues. She made a gentle joking reference to the hospital's endless supply of tissues, sharing with Maria a sense that there was an equality between them, which gave Maria 'permission' to cry. Maria needed to do this before she could talk. Whenever Maria looked up to say something, the nurse's manner was relaxed and open, signalling that she was receptive to Maria, and that she was not upset by the tears.

However, the nurse also added some remarks which showed that she understood Maria's emotions and behaviour, and how these related to her feelings about her face. When Maria said that she hated the way she looked, the helper reflected this back and asked her what it was about her face that she disliked. This was a close-ended question to give the helper some idea of Maria's tangible concerns about her face. Maria said that she hated most the loss of expression – that she could not smile. This led to further tears. The nurse waited for her to become calmer, and then said that not being able to smile must be hard for her when she was with other people. The nurse showed that she understood the social implications of this problem, and Maria felt she was being understood and that her difficulties were not being minimized. This comment also acted as a prompt which enabled her to talk more about her emotional reactions in social situations.

Maria felt ashamed of this outpouring of emotion and needed to feel that she had not been 'silly' and had not over-reacted. The nurse's calm and warm response to her tears was very accepting and helped Maria to feel more relaxed herself. If she had felt that she had made a fool of herself, she would not have returned, and her self-esteem would have taken a further blow. The helper recognized that Maria needed to express her pain which had been kept within her for so long, and this response allowed Maria to put her tears in the context of her needs, as something that she *needed* to do and which was part of the process of beginning to change. The nurse expressed her admiration for Maria's honesty and her ability to recognize her emotional state in this way, thus re-framing the tearfulness in a positive way. This helped Maria to feel good about the session and the part she had played in it. In a practical way, by providing tissues and by watching the time, the helper ensured that Maria had time during the session to calm down, and that she did not walk out with a tear-stained face.

Maria and the nurse did not rush to assess the problems and resources or to establish aims; that was left to the next time they met. To encourage Maria to focus on a way forward, the nurse suggested that Maria wrote down some of her main concerns before they met again, based on issues that had emerged in that first session. Thus the nurse made no interpretation, but encouraged Maria to begin the process of organizing her own concerns. Maria left saying that she felt much better for having talked, and that she had felt a huge weight had rolled off her as she talked.

The relationship that was established between Maria and the nurse was characterized by empathy and warmth. The nurse's unconditional acceptance of Maria was important as it allowed her to lose her feelings of shame about her reactions and to move forward to assess the problems and to bring about change. However, the nurse would need to ensure that the problems to be dealt with in this relationship were very clearly defined, as there was a potential danger that she could become involved in wider-ranging issues because she had been the first person Maria had been able to talk to so freely.

When the Adult is Reluctant to Talk: Agreeing a Basic Approach

People who have had a disfiguring injury may find it hard to express their emotions, particularly in a busy surgical unit where the focus tends to be on physical issues. This can be particularly true of those who are not used to talking about their feelings and who may view discussion about emotions as a sign of weakness.

John. He was 28 years old and worked in the engineering industry, using heavy industrial machinery. John lived with his girlfriend and her little boy. They had been together for two years. He considered himself to be the 'strong, silent type' and was rather scornful of the way his girlfriend talked about her feelings with her friends. He was involved in an accident at work when his right dominant hand was caught in a metal press and crushed. He had several operations, and was left with a hand that had a reasonably strong grip but was clumsy for fine movement. It was discoloured because of scars and skin grafts, and was misshapen. In addition, he had lost part of two fingers. The accident had happened three months before, and he had not yet returned to work, although he had recently been declared fit to do so. He was suffering mood swings and could be very irritable, arguing with his girlfriend, and not relating to her son. He felt very self-conscious about his hand because it looked and felt different, and would not look at it, but kept it covered with a glove, or in his pocket. As he was not using it, it was beginning to stiffen. The occupational therapist had become concerned about him and set time aside to talk with him in private about how he was coping.

At their first session, John was not communicative. He did not feel comfortable talking about his hand, and felt that he was there under pressure. The occupational therapist (OT) recognized that this issue needed to be discussed before they could move forward. He acknowledged John's sense of resistance by asking him why he thought he was there and what he wanted from the session. John said that he was only there because he had been told to come, but he could not see the point – he just wanted the OT to sort out his hand. He said that he saw no benefit in talking about things because it would make no difference to his hand.

The OT spent time discussing this with him. He did not dispute John's reactions and resisted the potential confrontation on the issue, moving from John's particular situation to a more general approach. He suggested that people did generally get on with their lives without having to talk to someone about their problems, but sometimes an unusual problem arose which needed a bit of extra help. He then moved back from the general to the personal, suggesting that John was having to deal with an unusually difficult situation. He had a severe hand injury and it was quite usual to seek extra help when dealing with this, to work out in what ways the situation might be improved. The OT also suggested that other members of John's family might be affected by the injury. Throughout this discussion, the OT talked with John in a straightforward way, avoiding jargon and treating him as an equal by allowing him to feel that this was something they needed to reach by common agreement.

Although John was initially suspicious, he did offer the information that he was concerned about the effect all this was having on his relationship with his girlfriend, and that he thought she might want to talk about it. Thus in the initial session, John was able to be less defensive. He had felt threatened by being offered this help, as he felt that it made him look weak, but when he was able to perceive it in a different and more positive way, particularly in relation to the stresses on his relationship with his girlfriend, he was able to accept that help. He agreed to return the following week in order to look at this issue, and the OT suggested that he bring his girlfriend with him.

The relationship between the OT and John was characterized by a practical approach and by a clear sense of contract which was developed before the helping relationship could move forward. John would only allow himself to move into a helping relationship with the OT when he understood its clearly defined limitations. The OT would need to work within these boundaries unless John identified other needs.

When the Adolescent Finds it Difficult to Talk: Establishing a Confidential Dialogue

It may be that the parents of a younger person feel that he or she is having problems coping with a disfigurement, but the young person may deny any difficulties. Perhaps this is because the young person does not have problems, and it is the parents who are troubled and having problems in coping. If this is the case, it would be appropriate to work with the parents rather than with the child. However, the child or adolescent may indeed be having real difficulties that are being denied. In this case, the helper is faced with the difficult problem of recruiting the adolescent to the helping process and encouraging that young person to talk through the problems in an open way. There is also the possibility that the young person feels the need to protect his or her parents if they seem upset, and has therefore kept the problems hidden and unspoken.

Sophie. Sophie was 15 years old. She had been born with a cranio-facial condition which affected the shape of her skull but not her intellectual abilities. She was an only child, as her parents felt so guilty and distressed when she was born that they felt unable to risk having more children. Sophie was always very close to her parents, who were very protective of her. She had had major surgery as a baby, and further more minor surgery before going to school. Since then, she had had no surgery, but her parents had been told that she could discuss further surgery when she was old enough to want it herself. Sophie was a slightly-built girl with blonde hair who was always dressed by her parents in pretty dresses, and who continued to wear clothes chosen by her mother. Her forehead was high, her eyes were rather far apart and bulged slightly and her nose was broad and rather thick. Her parents had become concerned about her because she seemed increasingly sad and withdrawn. She never went out socially, and was beginning to avoid family parties. She no longer talked to her parents, and spent her time alone in her room. At school, she was doing well, and was expected to go on to study A-levels, which would be at a Sixth Form College in another town. She had one close friend at school, a girl who was herself rather isolated. Her parents arranged for her to see the school counsellor.

Sophie was brought by her parents. Her mother was a quiet and anxious woman who became tearful recounting her reactions to the birth. She said that she had not taken photos of Sophie before the first operation because it would have been too distressing. She had always been very close to her daughter and thought they were 'like sisters', and became very upset and angry if anyone commented on her appearance or looked at her daughter in the street. She had not minded that Sophie was quiet and home-based, as she felt that was a safer place for her. However, she felt that Sophie was withdrawing from her, and that upset her. Sophie's father did not say anything, but was clearly upset and rather tearful. When encouraged to talk, he said that he felt very sorry for his daughter, and that he had always tried to do his best for her, but did not now know how to help her. Both parents expressed concerns about the coming exams and change of school. Sophie had grown up in a small town where all the children knew her, and they now worried that she would have difficulties going to a new environment.

Throughout this, Sophie listened but made no comment. Given her parents' distress, particularly that of her mother, it might be considered important to shield her from this by seeing the parents alone. However, that would have excluded Sophie and left her parents' discussion to her imagination. It would also have given her a child-like status, placing the power and control in the hands of the adults. Listening to her parents was part of the assessment process for her, and would be used later with her.

Her parents were then asked to leave whilst Sophie stayed to talk with the school counsellor. They sat in a quiet room with comfortable chairs, and Sophie could look out of the window from her chair. This allowed her to 'drop out' of the discussion and find a distraction when she felt she needed to. The counsellor recognized that Sophie was shy and found it difficult to talk freely, so she used the initial greeting period to talk more generally with Sophie about a recent school production, thus helping her to start talking.

The counsellor then began to talk about why they were there. She wanted to be honest and genuine with Sophie and to discuss the counselling situation with her. She summarized what Sophie's parents had said, but did not ask Sophie's opinion on this as this would have been to move to sensitive issues too quickly. She then discussed the establishment of a contract, and at this point she raised the issue of confidentiality. She stressed that everything that was said was confidential and would not be passed on to her parents. As the counsellor worked in the school she also needed to establish that no information would be passed on to anyone else in the school. For someone of Sophie's age, there may be issues that should be discussed with others, for example, talking about teasing with a teacher, or about family conflicts with her parents. Sophie was told that she could decide who was given information and that she was in control of this.

All helping relationships should be confidential. However, there are occasional exceptions to this. If information is revealed by a child or young person which suggests that they are at risk, for example, if sexual abuse is disclosed, then this information does need to be passed on to the relevant bodies, such as social services. This does not need to be talked through with the person when establishing confidentiality as it would raise unnecessary alarm, but only if and when it arose.

In discussing this contract, the counsellor also dealt with her perception that Sophie was reluctant to be there. Her parents had defined the problems from their perspective, but there was no indication from Sophie that she had chosen to see the counsellor. The counsellor was open and honest with Sophie, treating her in an equal way and not controlling her by setting the agenda. Having summarized what Sophie's parents had said, she asked her if she wanted to come along to discuss the way she saw things. At this point, the counsellor did not ask Sophie whether she had problems or what she wanted to talk about, or whether she agreed with her parents' assessment of the situation. All this would have been too much for Sophie to answer at this early stage, and could well have set up a defensive wall. She merely suggested that Sophie was welcome to come and talk. They agreed that they would meet up for two sessions and then decide where to go from there. The initial contract was a limited one to allow Sophie to decide whether this helping relationship had anything to offer her.

The school counsellor used her skills to allow Sophie a sense of equality in this relationship. She was open with her and gave her control to decide what to do next. She was genuine in her approach and responded to Sophie's hesitation by accepting her and by not imposing an adult perspective. She trusted Sophie to be able to decide for herself what she wanted to do, and Sophie responded to this by agreeing to come to see her again, thus demonstrating a sense of mutual trust.

Establishing a Helping Relationship with a Child

A child with a visible disfigurement may have problems which are separate from those of his or her parents, and although it is often possible to work through the parents rather than with the child, there are times when children need help which the parents find difficult to provide. This work involves establishing relationships with both the child and the parents. The child has particular needs as verbal communication may not always be the most effective or only means of interaction.

Matthew. This seven-year-old boy had been born with a bilateral cleft lip and palate which had affected his appearance, in that he had a flat nose and a scarred and rather thick upper lip. It had also affected his speech, and he spoke in an indistinct way. His hearing had been affected but this was corrected by grommets. After their initial shock, his parents had been able to accept and love him without difficulty, and everything went well for the first six years of his life. He had been to the local nursery school and then moved to the infants school with his friends, who accepted him. However, when he was eight he moved to the next school, and met many new children. He began to come home upset because he had been called names, such as 'fat lip' and 'alien'. A few children had started to pick on him and laugh at the way he talked. He had become angry and had got into a fight with one boy who was the prime leader in the teasing. It did no good, as he lost the fight and got into trouble with the teacher for fighting. He did not tell her why he had fought, and felt a sense of despair as things were out of control. He had recently had surgery to repair a small hole in the roof of his mouth in order to improve his speech, and had misunderstood what this surgery was about. He had told everyone at school that his lip was going to be made 'better', and was bitterly disappointed that it was unchanged. He was also anxious about returning to school looking the same. His parents spoke to the Special Needs teacher at the school and explained their concerns. She said she would spend time with him.

The teacher spent time getting to know Matthew, and did not immediately focus on his difficulties. She asked him what sort of things he liked doing, who he played with at school, how he spent his time outside school and with whom. Matthew discussed all this readily, and was clearly a child who was active and sociable. He had a computer at home on which he played games, and he also liked playing football and riding his bike. At school, he liked maths and drawing best. The teacher then asked him if he would do some drawings for her. She told him that it helped her to understand what he meant. She asked him to draw the people who lived in his house. He included the dog and the cat, and drew all his family members. When he drew himself, it was with the same face as his brother and sister, in a stylized child-like way. The teacher then asked him to do two more drawings. The first was him playing with his friends. He drew them playing football. She then asked him to draw himself at school with the children who were picking on him. He drew three people, himself, and two boys who were bigger and were raising their fists and had bubbles coming out of their mouths but with no words in them.

The teacher wanted to relate to Matthew and to encourage him to talk to her. She wanted to understand how he perceived the situation, and what he wanted to change. However, she knew that it might be difficult for him to discuss his problems immediately, and used his interest in drawing as a way of encouraging him to express himself. The fact that he drew his face as normal was not significant, as he was being asked to draw a situation and not specific detail. Although he was of the age when stylized drawings of the human figure are the norm, very few people would initially make any attempt to represent their own disfigurement unless they were specifically asked to draw themselves as a way of communicating about their self-image. It takes time to build up trust to expose feelings about the face. However, it might have been that Matthew was portraying the face he thought he was going to have. This would only emerge with time. The teacher told Matthew that they would do more drawings next time, and that they would talk about them. She showed him the folder in which she would be keeping the drawings. Thus he understood that the drawings had a purpose and would not be discarded.

Although some of the problems emerged in the initial contact between Matthew and the helper, the emphasis in these early stages was on the forming of a helping relationship rather than on looking at problems and setting aims. Although the teacher kept note of this information as being valuable in helping her to understand Matthew, the real purpose of this work was to build a sense of mutual interest between the two and to encourage Matthew to feel that he could communicate freely. The relationship was based on the teacher's unconditional regard for Matthew and her acceptance of what he had to say. It was also a genuine and honest relationship in that Matthew was clear about its purpose, which was to help him cope with problems relating to his disfigurement. He was thus able to differentiate this relationship from others with adults in school and outside of school.

Establishing a Relationship in a Crisis Situation

Sometimes disfigurement is the result of a traumatic accident such as a burn injury, and serious medical and surgical issues can dominate the early hospital treatment. However, it is important that potential problems are identified from the beginning so that help can be most effective. This means that the early relationship with the accident victim and the family will take place in an atmosphere of crisis.

Julie. This 12-year-old girl had been involved in a horrific house fire, caused by an electrical fault, when she was on her own in the house. She was rescued by neighbours, and taken to a specialist burns unit, where she was to spend the next three months. She had burns to her face and hands, and also to her chest. Her scalp had been burned and she had an area of permanent hair loss. She lived with her mother and older sister, both of whom were devastated by feelings of guilt and distress. She was quiet and rather withdrawn in the unit; she seemed to be coping, but she had had to go through painful treatment for her burns, including a daily bath to slough off the damaged skin. She suffered from early post-traumatic symptoms, and had recurring and frightening nightmares and flashbacks of the fire. Her mother blamed herself for leaving Julie alone in the house. Her older sister was doing badly at school and was very tearful.

The family were now faced with a major life crisis, and the hospital social worker was asked to see Julie. He needed to establish a relationship with Julie and the members of her family, and before going to meet Julie at the hospital for the first time, had a chance to see photos of her in her case notes. These were very shocking – Julie's face was swollen and black, with skin peeling off – but they helped prepare him for seeing Julie. He also spent time with the surgeon and nurses on the ward in order to understand Julie's treatment and what would be happening in the future, so that when he first met Julie he knew what to expect and had knowledge about the medical situation.

The burns unit was a daunting place, with lots of instruments and medical equipment, and nurses busy with patients. However, the social worker had arranged a time to meet Julie when things were quiet and she was not having any treatment, and the staff had explained to him what he could not touch because it was sterile. Julie was in a side ward and so he was able to close the door and have some private time with her. After explaining this to the ward sister, he put a hand-written notice saying 'Do not enter' on the door to ensure that they were not interrupted. If she had been on the ward, he would have drawn the curtains firmly around the bed. However, everything said on a main ward is overheard by those around, and any communication would have to be confined to introductions. If faced with that situation, it would be better to find a side ward to go to for discussion.

The social worker introduced himself to Julie who was lying on her bed, and sat down next to her so that they were at about the same height. Because he had prepared himself for what she would look like, he was not shocked and was able to greet her in a normal and friendly way. The normality of his response was important for their relationship as it signalled an acceptance of her as an individual rather than as a burns victim. He introduced himself and talked to her about why he was there – to help her and her family in any way he could. He talked in a general way about the hospital, about her cards and flowers and about the poster on her wall, and did not launch immediately into the problems. This situation can seem so overwhelming that the helper has a particular need to establish a calm and friendly relationship. There would be plenty of time to work together in the future; at this stage and in this setting the helper needs to relate to the individual in a friendly and accepting way.

The social worker then addressed immediate issues. He asked Julie whether there was anything that worried her just then, and she said that she missed her mother. It seemed that Julie's mother had been avoiding coming because she became so upset. He arranged to meet her mother and sister at home, away from the hospital atmosphere. After listening to them and observing their distress, he decided that he would need help as the family's problems were so acute and diverse, and asked a colleague to work with him and see Julie's mother and sister. He saw that Julie's mother needed support to work through her initial emotional responses so that she could see her daughter without too much upset.

The social worker also made contact with Julie's school and talked with her form teacher. He arranged for the teacher to come to see Julie, first preparing her for what she would see. They agreed that she would keep in touch and give some work to Julie when it was appropriate.

Thus the early encounters were with many people in Julie's world, in order to ensure that Julie had support and as much continuity in her life as possible. The social worker was also able to form a friendly and helpful relationship with Julie without any intervention apart from helping others communicate. He knew that there would be work to do in the future but that this would become apparent as time went on.

When a Baby is Born with a Visible Difference: Working with Parents

When a baby is born with a marked facial disfigurement, the parents may find it difficult to adjust (see Chapter 2). In this situation, the helper will be establishing a relationship with the parents rather than with the child.

Andrew and Tracy (parents of Jonathan). This young couple had everything going for them. Tracy became pregnant as planned, and the pregnancy went well. When their son was born, he had a small mark on his face. Over the next few weeks and months, this grew dramatically in size and was diagnosed as a facial haemiangioma. It was a dark red and raised birthmark, covering the side of his nose and part of his cheek. The plastic surgeon they consulted told them that it was now at its worst and would gradually improve, in that the discoloration would go down over the years. She said that the best treatment was to do nothing but wait until he was older and the colour had largely gone, and then they would consider whether there was anything further to do. The parents were very upset about this and were having great problems dealing with the responses of others. Their family told them that they should insist on treatment, and go abroad for it if necessary. Their friends and acquaintances were shocked and agreed with the family. Strangers would stare at Jonathan in his pram and ask Tracy what she had done to him. For Tracy, this was the hardest to bear, as she felt that she was being criticized by the rest of the world. She became angry with the surgeon and desperate for treatment which would remove the haemiangioma. They went to see other experts in surgery and laser treatment but were always given the same advice. They began to consider going to the United States. This went on for the early years of Jonathan's life. When he was three years old, the surgeon recommended that they talk with their health visitor. They were at first very resistant, as they felt that they were being labelled as hysterical parents. However, as they recognized that they were under stress, they did agree reluctantly.

The health visitor saw Andrew and Tracy at their home. She felt that this would be more acceptable to them, as it was on their own territory and away from the hospital environment. At this session, Jonathan was with his grandmother. The parents were on the defensive, and talked to the health visitor mainly about Jonathan's medical history. This led her to clarify her role as she talked with them, explaining that she was not there to discuss what surgeons and others had done or not done, but to help them cope with the situation as best they could. She suggested that she could offer help in three ways:

1) By talking with them about their feelings about Jonathan's face and giving them the chance to talk through their concerns;
2) By helping them deal with the responses of others to Jonathan's face;
3) By helping them to work out the best way of handling Jonathan's developing awareness of his face.

Tracy then became very upset. She had been worried about all this, and had displaced her emotions and energy into the fight for treatment to remove the mark on Jonathan's face. Although she would not let go of the hope that something physical could be done, she recognized that she needed help with her emotional state. Andrew said that they would not need help to deal with the responses of others once the mark had been removed, but he felt Tracy needed some support, and it might be a good idea for her to meet the health visitor.

By being clear about her role and what she had to offer to this couple in terms of help, the health visitor was able to overcome their initial defensiveness and establish a relationship with them. This also ensured that she was not closely associated in their minds with the surgeon, and prevented their concerns about treatment taking over the agenda.

Both Tracy and Andrew needed help in their different ways. Tracy was distressed and tearful and wanted support and the chance to talk things through. Andrew also needed help, but was still fixed in the medical mode, and was rigid and defensive in his belief about the efficacy of surgery or laser treatment. It was important for them as a couple that Tracy was not identified as the one who was not coping. The health visitor suggested to them that it would be helpful to them both if she saw them together, and Tracy said that she would also prefer Andrew to be there. Tracy asked him if he would take time off work to do this, and he said he would, in order to support her. At this stage, he could not accept that he needed help, and the health visitor did not challenge this. However, she prepared the way for the helping process with these parents by ensuring that both would be involved. It was agreed that these sessions would be at their home, and on a weekly basis at first. It was also agreed that Jonathan would not be present, as he was old enough to overhear and too young to be included in the discussion. This also protected him from any negative comments they might need to make. Thus they were all able to agree an initial contract that specified what areas they would be covering, and that both parents came.

Conclusion

The quality of the helping relationship is of crucial importance in the helping process. The early days of that relationship can be decisive in determining whether such a relationship has been formed. The helper does need to have the ability and the knowledge to use his or her personal qualities and skills, particularly when working in the health field where the individuals may be experiencing physical problems and may be reluctant to ask for help in coping. The following chapters carry forward the case studies in order to look in detail at ways of developing the helping relationship.

SUMMARY

❑ The relationship between the helper and the individual begins at their first meeting. Working in the field of disfigurement, there are certain characteristic patterns to this first meeting.

❑ When the adult needs to talk: the person may be very distressed and tearful, and express a sense of shame. The warmth and acceptance by the helper in this situation allows trust to develop.

❑ When the adult is reluctant to talk: those seeking physical treatment may be reluctant to accept any other form of help. The initial contract should be clearly established based on clear aims and equality within the relationship.

❑ When the adolescent finds it difficult to talk: the adolescent is often very defensive and may not have chosen to come. The parents may need to be offered alternative help from another source, and the adolescent encouraged to develop a confidential dialogue with the helper.

❑ Establishing a helping relationship with a child: children may find it difficult to express their concerns in a verbal way, and other means such as drawing and play can be used to establish a relationship.

❑ Establishing a helping relationship in a crisis situation: those with traumatic disfigurement may be seriously ill, and the family profoundly affected. The helper needs to manoeuvre through the physical treatment to ensure early needs are met.

❑ When a baby is born with a visible difference: the birth of a baby with disfigurement can precipitate a problem of adjustment for the parents, and the helper needs to understand their reactions when establishing the relationship.

6

Meeting the Needs: Identifying Problems and Setting Aims

Once the initial encounter has helped to establish the relationship, the helper can work with the individual to identify problems and then set aims in the context of personal resources. It is important to focus on strengths as well as difficulties, particularly when the difficulties seem overwhelming.

Identifying Problems

Maria. After her initial and highly charged emotional encounter with the liaison nurse, Maria returned the following week for a further session. The nurse had suggested that she write down some of her principle concerns. and Maria brought with her a long document, as the session had stirred up a lot of memories and feelings she wanted to record. Together with the nurse, she used this to identify her main concerns. They went through what she had written and underlined every mention of unhappy feelings. The situations relating to these feelings were then highlighted and the writing was used to extract particular events which caused unhappiness or distress. Maria was encouraged to put together those events which caused similar difficulties for her. She was then asked to rank them in order of difficulty, starting with the worst problem. Thus from a mass of writing, the nurse helped Maria to focus on specific problems. These were:

- *Her feelings of shame and loss of self-worth.* These robbed her of her confidence and had made her apprehensive with others. Maria described her sense of being stigmatized by the disfigurement; her external and visible difference had also made her feel as though she was different as a person. She had internalized her feelings of looking different and experienced this as a sense of inferiority, which caused her to cry at home when she was alone.

- *Difficulties in social encounters.* There are different levels of social encounters – with family and friends, with acquaintances and with strangers. Maria felt safe with her own family, who were a source of strength, and found encounters with acquaintances the most problematic. She felt uncomfortable with strangers, which made her vulnerable, affecting her everyday life. This concern about casual acquaintances is commonly associated with self-consciousness, and would be anticipated in this situation; it arises from a fear of being compared to the way one looked before.
- *Decision-making about surgery.* Maria felt that she was not strong enough to cope with such a decision. Whenever she thought about it, she became tearful and she did not know whether she was emotionally strong enough to go through the operation, or how she would respond to her changed appearance after surgery. The prospect of reconstructive surgery had precipitated a crisis for her. This is generally a sign that there are unresolved issues which need to be dealt with before considering this decision.
- *Problems in her relationship with her husband.* Maria put this after the others, because she felt that this was not relevant to the problems of disfigurement. However, she did recognize that many of the difficulties over the years had been a result of her emotional responses to disfigurement. Although Maria did not put this as her major concern, it is serious. Social and family support is of crucial importance in coping with stressful life events, and the withdrawal of that support makes coping difficult. For most people, the partner is the primary source of support. In addition, the feelings of her husband's rejection reinforced Maria's own sense of shame.

Because the nurse had worked to establish an unconditional acceptance in the initial encounter, Maria felt able to talk with her about her problems and still feel accepted. The writing was a useful way for someone like Maria, who enjoyed writing, to express her feelings and problems away from the session, and it also meant that the nurse was able to use this within the session to extract what was most relevant to the helping process.

John. John's girlfriend came with him to the next session with the OT. She was very concerned about him, and said that she felt he had been changed by his injury. The OT asked them to talk about the last week and to identify any difficulties that had arisen. John's girlfriend was more forthcoming than he was, and described events which had concerned her. The OT encouraged them to talk about these events, and to consider what role John's hand injury and his reactions to it had played in them. This placed the focus on specific events and generated explanations about the impact of the injury on these events. The concerns they identified together were:

- *John's altered emotional state.* He had been irritable all week and felt that he was 'on a short fuse'. He had vivid memories of his hand being crushed, and was still disturbed by nightmares and flashbacks about this. He also found it difficult to concentrate on anything. These are all typical post-traumatic symptoms and this was identified as a problem for both of them individually, and also for their relationship together.
- *John's reluctance to return to work.* He found it very difficult to contemplate the idea of going back to work on the same machinery. The memories of the injury were so vivid that he felt he had to avoid any reminders of it. This was identified as a problem for John.
- *John's self-consciousness about his hand.* He avoided looking at his hand and could not accept it or re-integrate its changed appearance into his body image. Because he was unable to accept it himself, he could not imagine that anyone else would. The appearance of the hand acted as a trigger to his distress about his injury. There was another consequence for him in that he felt uncomfortable touching his girlfriend with his hand, and this was inhibiting their sexual relationship. This was identified as a problem for both of them.
- *The general effect on their relationship.* John and his girlfriend had been very close before the injury, but she now found it difficult to deal with his moods and the effect of his self-consciousness on their intimacy. In addition, she could not understand why he was so reluctant to return to work, and was becoming worried about their financial situation. She was also concerned about the effect his emotional state was having on her son. He felt that she was not able to understand him, and all this created tension between them. This was identified as a problem for them both.

By identifying who was affected, it became clear that the injury had an impact on both John and his girlfriend. This reinforced the initial contract, as it became increasingly clear that the difficulties he was having were affecting their relationship in many ways.

Sophie. Sophie had been reluctant to admit to any difficulties, and so it required sensitive help to encourage her to identify her problems. The counsellor used a technique developed by construct therapists

(Fransella and Dalton, 1990) known as *self-characterization*. The counsellor said that she wanted to know more about Sophie and so she would ask her to talk about herself in the third person, as though she was Emma, a good friend of Sophie's. The counsellor asked her to suppose Emma was there and she was not. What did Sophie think Emma would say to the counsellor about her, how would she describe her, what sort of person she is, what she likes, what she doesn't like, what makes her laugh, what makes her sad. What would Emma say? Thus the self-characterization began with the words 'Sophie is ...'. The counsellor wrote down every word that Sophie said. Sophie, talking through her friend, described herself as being generally quite happy, but sometimes having the following problems.

- *Dislike of her appearance: Sophie wishes that she looked more attractive. She wants surgery to look like she feels inside. She wants to look like everyone else.* Sophie was showing signs that she was going through difficulties in accepting her face. The only way she could cope at the moment was to hold on to a belief in a magic resolution, and that the fantasized lost face was waiting to be restored to her. These reactions often occur in adolescence and they mirrored her mother's difficulties in adjusting to Sophie's appearance. The family had all held on to the belief that there was some surgical resolution.
- *Anxiety about the future: Sophie is worried about going to Sixth Form College. She will have to make new friends. People may not like her because of how she looks.* Like her parents, Sophie felt worried about how she would cope at the Sixth Form College. She would not admit to any social difficulties, although she did say that she felt happiest with people she knew well and did not feel comfortable meeting new people. Adolescents are naturally defensive and it has been found that those who have visible anomalies are particularly defensive about any other problems. It is best assessed by discussing with them in a positive way who they spend their time with and how they spend their leisure time.
- *Her parents: Sophie's mum and dad are great, but sometimes they are too worried about her and won't let her grow up.* For some adolescents with visible disfigurement, the greatest obstacle they have to deal with is gaining their independence from their protective parents. However, Sophie recognized that it was difficult for them if they thought she would be upset, such as when going shopping amongst strangers by herself. She felt that she had never really been able to talk to them about any worries because they would get upset. Sophie had picked up the stigmatizing implications of her parents over-

protectiveness, and she felt that she was not seen as competent by them. However, she remained reliant on them for her main support, and was dependent on their emotional responses and their judgement.

As far as Sophie was concerned, the most pressing problem was her struggle to establish some independence. However, she recognized that this would require her to develop her own ways of coping with the outside world unprotected by her parents. She felt that her dislike of her face was too difficult to deal with, and anyway could only be resolved by surgery. She also felt that she would feel less anxious about the future if she could be more independent.

Julie. It was difficult to establish a relationship with Julie at first as she was so non-communicative and withdrawn. The social worker came regularly and talked with her at home, gradually winning her trust, and beginning the process of identifying problems. These emerged over a period of time and mainly from his own observations. He was able to witness what was happening and to see the ways in which this was affecting those concerned. As he observed them, he reflected these back to Julie and her family in a gentle way, acknowledging the problems with them. He identified the problems for Julie as follows.

- *Problems in adjusting to her changed appearance.* Julie found it very difficult to look at her face in the mirror, and had asked that the mirrors in the house be removed. She did not like to look at her hands and kept them covered with bandages. She had recently been measured for pressure garments for her hands and trunk, and looked forward to having them as they covered the burns. She found it very difficult to talk about this, and became tearful whenever she did. Julie's disfiguring injuries were very traumatic for her; they had come at a time when her body was beginning to change from that of a child to that of an adolescent, and thus when her body image was unstable. She would almost certainly experience feelings of bereavement for the loss of her previous appearance, and for adolescents at this unstable time, the loss of appearance can become the loss of self. By refusing to look at herself, she was trying to maintain denial as a self-protective strategy so that she would not feel the overwhelming sense of grief and loss. However, this cannot be sustained indefinitely.
- *Her social isolation.* Julie had refused to see any of her friends, and could not imagine how she would ever go back to school. She spent her days watching television at home on her own as her mother

worked shifts and could only be at home for part of the day, and her sister was at school. She would not go out apart from trips to the hospital, and always covered herself with dressings when she did so.

- *Missed schooling.* Julie was not very successful at school, and was anxious about all the work she was missing. She also missed the social contact of school and was bored at home. Interruption to education is one of the major problems for children who have suffered severe trauma. They miss many months following the injury while they are treated for the acute effect of the burns, and then miss more school when they have further treatment.

- *The continuing treatment.* Julie had suffered during her treatment, and had developed an anxiety about further surgery. In particular she had developed a phobic response to needles. Julie would find it difficult to make any decisions about surgery in her present state. She was too frightened of the treatment, and her denial meant that she could not consider objectively what needed to be done.

- *The reactions of the family.* Her mother and sister were not coping with all this, and could not provide any support for her. Julie was worried about them and felt some responsibility for them.

By observing the situation and discussing what he observed with Julie, the social worker was able to identify problems which would focus the helping relationship.

The SWOT Analysis: A Way of Identifying Problems and Resources

Within the context of effective and skilled listening, there are various techniques which are useful in the identification of problems and resources. The SWOT analysis, used in management training and assessment, is one such technique. This is always carried out as a joint activity by the individual and the helper, and stands for **S**trengths, **W**eaknesses, **O**pportunities and **T**hreats.

To illustrate this, a SWOT analysis was done with John, a young businessman with a successful career in banking at the time of a road traffic accident. He was married, with no children as yet, and his family lived nearby. As a result of the accident he suffered extensive fractures to his face, and was left with a sunken eye and some scarring. His face felt strange to him because of nerve and tissue damage, and when he smiled, there was slight distortion of his mouth.

Strengths: the helper worked with John to identify his strengths. This was done by asking him whom he would turn to for support and what kind of support he could expect from family and friends. The helper identified particular people in his support network by name, and talked through what support they could offer and how John would go about getting this support; for example, would he phone them, or write to them, or perhaps ask another member of the family to approach them? By doing this, the helper encouraged John to turn to his usual support network. If John had not been used to gaining support from others, then it would have been useful to ask him to list who was the most approachable person he knew and the person to whom he could talk most freely.

In addition, the helper discussed with John how he characteristically solved problems, and encouraged him to remember how he had tackled difficulties in the past. It was also important to elicit from John his own sense of personal commitment to overcoming his problems and to ask him how optimistic he felt in being able to do this. Following this initial work the helper was able to summarize John's strengths with him. These were:

- *supportive wife and family;*
- *problem-solving ability;*
- *personal drive to overcome his problems.*

Weaknesses: the helper then looked with John at what might work against him in overcoming his problems, for example, whether there were any pressures at home or at work which made things difficult. John identified potential career difficulties and lack of support at work. His company put a lot of pressure on him, and he had unsupportive and competitive colleagues.

Opportunities: It is always useful to consider what potential benefits can be gained from a situation and from learning how to cope with it. The helper did this by discussing with John what he would gain by working through his problems and resolving them. This required John to consider what skills he needed to develop to cope with his situation and how this would be of general benefit to him. He decided that he could learn assertiveness and increased social skills, and could improve his relationship with people close to him, based on a new awareness of the need to strengthen these relationships.

Threats: as the final part of the SWOT analysis, the helper worked with John to identify potential problems which could arise as a result of his injury. These were not yet problems, but could become so in the future. The helper asked John what his fears were about the future, and summarized these as potential threats: career problems; increasing self-consciousness about his face.

John was drawing on family and personal resources, but had to contend with social and work pressures, as well as his own feelings about his face. The SWOT analysis would be an appropriate approach to the setting of aims for John, who works in the world of management and is familiar with this approach. It normalizes the situation and makes it more acceptable to him. The focus is on both positive and negative issues and does not dwell on problems, but neither does it mask difficulties. Above all, it is action-oriented, and leads naturally to a discussion about what is to be aimed for, and what resources can be used to achieve this.

Setting the Aims

Once the problems have been identified, then the helping process moves forward to set aims which will be linked to these problems and will focus the process of helping, identifying the person's resources which will help in the achievement of these aims.

Maria. Once Maria had identified her problems, she worked with the nurse to identify short-, medium- and long-term aims. The nurse helped her to do this by encouraging her to talk about what she wanted to achieve and what she wanted to be different. They worked together to link the aims specifically to the problems which had been identified. This approach is particularly important when the situation seems overwhelming, as in Maria's case.

The situation:
'Tell me about something that has happened recently that has gone wrong, related to your disfigurement.'
'I went into a shop to buy a sofa, but felt really embarrassed when the assistant asked me if I had had an accident. I felt terrible and ran out without buying anything'.

The problem: The helper then encouraged Maria to recognize what was familiar in that situation and whether she could pick out any general issues.
'What had gone wrong? Had this happened before? Was there a recurring pattern here?'
'Whenever this happens, I don't know what to say or do. I hate others to mention my face. It always upsets me when they do. I feel humiliated that they have noticed my face and that they are passing judgement on me'.

The consequences: The helper then moved the discussion forward to consider what followed from this in terms of her behaviour and her emotional state each time she experienced this sense of public humiliation.

'How did this make you behave at the time? Do these situations have any longer-term effect for you?'

Short-term: Maria felt tearful and her behaviour was out of control. She failed to get what she wanted, and was angry with herself for her responses.

Long-term: Maria was disinclined to go back to this place or others like it. She decided to buy through mail order, thus decreasing her contact with others. She also felt increasingly depressed at her sense of helplessness and ineffectiveness.

Aims:

At this point, Maria and the helper identified aims based on these problems:

- **Short-term:** to identify what is going wrong in difficult social situations;
- **Medium-term:** to develop strategies for coping with these situations;
- **Long-term:** to be able to lead a more active social life and mix more freely with others.

They then considered what personal and social resources she had to help her to achieve these aims.

The resources: The next stage was to look more positively at Maria's personal strengths, how she had dealt with other problems not connected to her disfigurement, and what social support she had or could build. Thus the helper encouraged her to focus on her resources.

'Tell me what works well for you in your life. What makes you happy? What do you do well?'

'I organize events for a local charity, mainly by phone. I can relate well to others on the phone. I can also persuade people to part with their money! I have a close relationship with my children, and I like writing and thinking things through.'

Thus she was encouraged to recognize her ability to be assertive when she needed to be, her strengths as a mother and her intelligence and problem-solving abilities.

On the basis of this work, a joint decision was made to concentrate initially on dealing with social encounters. This would allow for practical work where progress could be seen, and she felt that if she could achieve some control over this area, it might help her to feel more worthwhile. It was decided to postpone the surgical issue, and also her relationship problems with her husband, as both of these seemed too overwhelming and threatening to her at this point.

John. John and his girlfriend had recognized that there were problems which affected them both. The next stage was to set aims as part of the agreed contract. The OT encouraged John to identify his aims by linking them to their problems. For each of these problems, they reached agreement about what John wanted to achieve. Once he had agreed his long-term aim, the OT helped him to consider what he would need to aim for in order to get there. Thus in terms of his self-consciousness about his hand, they identified the following aims:

- **Short-term:** to be able to look at his hand more easily and not to hide it from himself;
- **Medium-term:** to be able to let others see it, and to feel comfortable when he touched his girlfriend;
- **Long-term:** to accept the final appearance of the hand as part of him.

Together with the OT, the couple identified John's strengths with some particular help from his girlfriend. These were:

- *their love for each other;*
- *John's hard-working approach to life;*
- *John's sense of humour.*

Sophie. The school counsellor had carried out a self-characterization with Sophie in order to identify the problems, which were then linked to aims. Once the problems have been identified, it is easier to look at aims because they become an alternative to the problem. For example, Sophie had said that she was unhappy about her appearance. The counsellor was then able to ask her what would be the alternative to being unhappy about this. When Sophie said it was to be happy about her appearance, the counsellor used her knowledge of the principles in setting aims to qualify this. Being happy about an abnormal appearance may not be attainable for Sophie, but accepting her appearance as part of her might be more possible; this becomes a long-term aim.

In order to achieve this, short- and medium-term aims are generated, based on the question 'What do you need to achieve in order to adjust to your appearance?'. Deciding in a realistic way about further surgery may be a reasonable shorter-term aim.

Each long-term aim related to a specific problem. Thus in terms of the issue of her parents and her ability to cope with a more independent and less protected life, Sophie decided on the following aims.

- **Short-term:** to establish areas in which she wanted to be more independent and to work out ways of developing this independence, particularly being able to get out and about;
- **Medium-term:** to practise coping strategies and to become more independent without hurting her parents;
- **Long-term:** to feel confident that she could cope alone.

Together with the school counsellor, she discussed what she had which could help her achieve these aims. Her strengths were:

- *Her intelligence and success at school.* This helped her solve problems and also gave her a sense of achievement and self-esteem.
- *The love and support of her parents.* Thus her parents were both a problem *and* a strength.
- *Her desire to be more independent.*

She recognized that her parents might need support, and that they had their own problems and distress. She was relieved by the suggestion that they might benefit from counselling separately from her, as this took some of the burden away from her.

Julie. Once Julie's main problems had been identified, it became easier to consider aims. The social worker ensured that they try to establish immediate and specific aims, as Julie's problems could become overwhelming. They looked at what she wanted to achieve in the long-term, and that took some discussion. When the social worker asked her what she most wanted to change right now, she said that she wanted to get her life back to normal. The social worker respected this and helped her to consider what she should aim for in order to achieve that longer-term aim.

- **Short-term:** to cope with specific problems such as the interruption to her education;
- **Medium-term:** to help Julie develop strategies for coping;
- **Long-term:** for Julie and her family to be able to live a fulfilling life without professional intervention.

When they discussed what made her happy, she talked about her friends with great enthusiasm. They visited her regularly and the social worker could observe the warmth of those relationships. He recognized through observation and talking to family and to teachers at school that she was someone who got on well with others and had grown up in a happy and sociable family. Thus they found that her strengths were:

- *her open and friendly nature and her positive life-experience;*
- *the support of school and friends.*

The process of identifying problems and resources and setting aims can take time, and there is no value in attempting to bring about change when there is no clear agreement about what needs to be changed. The process of carrying out this work plays a role in developing the relationship, and sets the scene for working together as equal partners.

SUMMARY

❏ The process of identifying problems and setting aims needs to be carried out before the main work of helping can begin.

❏ The process is based on the principles of skilled helping, such as non-judgemental acceptance, skilled listening, warmth and mutual regard.

❏ It may be necessary to draw in other people to gather information, but the problems and aims should always be those of the individual.

❏ Ways of defining problems and setting aims include *keeping a diary, talking together with relatives and friends, self-characterizations* and *SWOT analysis.*

❏ Aims should be clear, realistic and closely linked to the problems.

❏ Resources should be clearly identified, as these will have a major effect on the ability of the individual to cope with disfigurement. It may be necessary to develop these resources, such as family and social support, in order to bring about change.

7

Meeting the Needs: Working Together to Achieve the Aims

Once an initial relationship has been established and agreement has been reached on problems and aims, the helper needs to consider how he or she can most effectively work with the individual to achieve those aims. The problems described in Chapter 2 will be used as the framework for this chapter, and the case histories will be used to illustrate the strategies for helping.

Coping with Social Encounters

Many people with a visible disfigurement become aware that others are responding to them in a way which is influenced by that disfigurement. It can be useful to clarify whether these people are strangers, acquaintances and/or friends, and then to work together to find strategies for coping.

Maria. In order to look closely at the social issue, and to identify exactly what happened which made life difficult, Maria agreed to keep a diary for two weeks. She was asked to record the following information:

- *social encounters which were difficult;*
- *when and where they happened;*
- *what the person said or did;*
- *what she said or did;*
- *what her thoughts and feelings were about the encounter.*

The helper read through the diary with Maria at the next session in order to ensure she understood what Maria had written. The most frequent problem was taking the children to their activities, when she felt that she tried to avoid talking to the other mothers because of her embarrassment. She assumed that they were critical of her, and she felt ashamed in front of her children. She felt that it would have been easier if they knew what was wrong with her face, as this made things easier with her family and close friends. However, she did not want to make a big thing of it.

With the nurse, Maria picked out each time she had automatically had a negative belief about the responses of others, and accepted the possibility that she might have misinterpreted the responses of these people. She told the nurse what she would have liked to have said to them, and then together they modified it into a script which was appropriate to the situation, and with which she felt comfortable. She decided to use the forthcoming surgery as a way into this. Her script was that she should start a conversation talking about the children they were watching. As the opportunity arose, she should say that her daughter would be going to her grandparents when she had further surgery to her face. She would then give an explanation of what had happened without making any comments about her own emotional responses unless asked. She would keep it as factual as possible, and downplay her own responses which seemed appropriate in this context.

Together with the liaison nurse, she went through a rehearsal of this, with the nurse taking the role of the other person. They sat together as though they were watching children playing. The nurse made some conversation about the children. Maria then started talking about them going to their grandparents because she was going into hospital. The nurse showed curiosity, and Maria started talking about the surgery. When she got stuck, the nurse briefly took Maria's role and said what she thought that Maria wanted to say. This switching of roles should always be brief, and based on a careful listening and empathic understanding, as it is very important that the nurse does not create her own script, thus taking control away from the person with disfigurement. By practising this with the nurse, Maria felt more prepared to carry it out.

The following session was two weeks later. Maria had found an opportunity to try using this new way of handling social encounters, but was unsure about how successful she had been. She had felt very anxious talking about it, and thought that she had been too emotional. When asked how the other person had reacted, she recognized that she was so preoccupied with her own responses that she had not noticed the other person's reactions. This was an important learning point for her. Despite her apprehension, she felt a sense of relief at having broached the subject, and felt more at ease as a result.

This had been a hard task, in that it made Maria talk about something she found very difficult. But having done so, she felt more in control and her sense of having achieved this improved her self-esteem. She realized that her preoccupation with herself meant she could not monitor the reactions of others. While Maria felt that she could have another go at this task, she also felt that her anxiety before talking had got in the way. The nurse suggested that she could develop strategies to deal with that anxiety and the rest of the session was taken up with showing Maria simple breathing control exercises (see Box 1), which she could do when she began to experience anticipatory anxiety.

Box 1: Breathing control exercises

1) Take a short breath in and then SIGH out your breath with your mouth slightly open so that your rib cage and your shoulders go down.

2) Pause, and then breathe in steadily through your mouth, counting 'one and two and three and four'.

3) Pause and then sigh out your breath again, making sure that you empty your lungs.

4) Pause, and then breathe in again as before.

Keep going until you feel calmer.

If you are in a public place and if sighing would be too noticeable, just breathe out steadily through slightly parted lips. It can help to visualize that you are 'cleaning out' your lungs, breathing out black smoky air and breathing in pure cold air. Practise this at home sitting in front of a mirror so that you can see the effect of the shoulders and rib cage going down.

Maria grew more confident talking with other women, whom she came to realize were usually sympathetic. At the same time, she felt more confident in herself. She found the breathing control exercises useful, and also learnt additional ways of relaxing in tense situations (see Box 2 overleaf). These strategies helped her to feel more in control of herself, and allowed her to develop ways of talking to people she knew.

The next stage was to deal with feelings of self-consciousness with strangers. Maria found it difficult to walk down the street, or into a crowded shop. Together with the nurse, she developed the strategies in Box 3 (overleaf).

Box 2: Other methods of relaxation

1) Bring your shoulders down with your back straight, so that the distance from your ears to your shoulders grows longer, and then relax your shoulders. *Maria was inclined to hunch herself defensively against her feelings of threat, and suffered from pains at the back of her head.*

2) Stretch your fingers and hands, and then let them relax. *Maria tended to clench her hands when she was tense.*

Box 3: Strategies for dealing with feelings of self-consciousness with strangers

1) Walking down the street with your eyes out of focus, so that you don't see anybody's face. *This allowed Maria to hide from others while going about her daily life. She found that if she did not look, then she did not know whether anyone was looking at her. This is a useful avoiding strategy as people do not always want to deal with the issue of being looked at.*

2) Holding the eye of shop assistants and smiling. *This is a way of helping the other person to overcome their feeling of embarrassment. Smiling allows the other person to smile back, thus establishing a non-threatening atmosphere. The behaviour of the other person is often characterized by anxiety, and not knowing how to respond, which can make them look frowning and critical. They may also stare. By taking the initiative, the person with disfigurement helps to manage the encounter. Although Maria's smile was rather distorted by her facial palsy, it was still apparent that she was smiling, and the smile of the other person encouraged her to feel that her face was moving appropriately.*

3) Going through a day-time visualization. *Maria did this when she was sitting somewhere, such as on the bus, and could feel other people looking at her. She would visualize something pleasant, like an excerpt from a film she had seen, set on a beautiful island – 'day-dreaming', but in a deliberate way.*
    This strategy allows the person with disfigurement to cut off from the stares of others over a sustained period. It can be combined with breathing control and relaxation if the person's anxiety is too high to allow the visualization to take place.

Maria found that as she grew more comfortable talking with acquaintances, she was also more able to deal with strangers, as she recognized that their judgement of her might not necessarily be critical. She was able to consider alternative possibilities, for example, that they could be interested in her in a kindly way, or that they might not really be looking at all. Thus the progress she made in changing her own attitude and behaving in a more positive way with acquaintances also helped her cope with strangers. Whenever she felt particularly vulnerable with strangers, she would use one of the strategies described in Box 3.

Sophie. Sophie had become very concerned about what others might think of her appearance and became very anxious when anyone looked at her. The school counsellor suggested that she keep a diary recording any daily events that were difficult, why she thought they had happened and how she responded to them. The format of the diary is shown in Box 4. It was kept intentionally simple and non-directive, as it allowed her to say as much or as little as she wanted, but encouraged her to identify the links between what happened and what her responses were, particularly the cognitive component – what she thought about it. The second column, why she thought it had happened, is important as it helps understand the attributions that she makes, that is, what her understanding and beliefs are about the cause of events.

Box 4: Diary extracts			
What happened	**Why Sophie thought it had happened**	**What she did**	**What she felt and thought about it**
Going to school on the bus and was stared at by some younger children.	Because her face looked strange and ugly.	Turned face away and let her hair fall over her face.	Felt hot and bothered and felt her heart pounding – wished she looked different.

Sophie came back two weeks later with her diary. The example given in Box 4 was one of her entries. Generally, she seemed very aware of anyone looking at her and always attributed it to negative responses to her face. This diary formed the basis of her discussions with the counsellor over the next few sessions. As they went through it, she was encouraged to consider whether (a), there was any other reason why the event might have occurred, and (b), was there any other way she might have responded. Some events were unambiguous, and it was obvious that people were reacting in a negative way to her face. However, on other occasions, there were alternative explanations. An example of this was when she walked into a cafe and people looked up as she entered. The counsellor suggested that they might look up when anyone went in, and that they were only showing a general interest. She found that hard to accept and did not feel that anyone else was looked at in the same way as she was. It was agreed that she would meet with the school counsellor for a coffee in a town-centre cafe during the week. Because of her fixed beliefs, it was difficult for her to generate any possible alternative responses. Sophie and the counsellor met in the cafe and spent time observing other people. Because Sophie was so wrapped up in her own concerns, and because of her immaturity and lack of independent relationships with her peers, she was self-centred in her preoccupations and could not really understand others. She also tended to keep her head down and her face averted and thus did not see other people clearly. As they watched the other people in the cafe, Sophie recognized that people did look up when someone came in.

This was an important learning process for Sophie, and helped her to begin to question her fixed and negative beliefs. It allowed her to begin to generate alternative beliefs and thoughts about what had happened. She said that she did not know whether they were true, but agreed that when she was not sure of the reason why something had happened, it was better for her confidence to focus on more positive possibilities and take a more optimistic view.

The next stage was to consider her reactions to unambiguous events, for example, when she overheard someone say to her friend, 'Look at her, what's wrong with her face?' In order to deal with these sorts of comments, she needed to develop strategies which would either protect her in a defensive way, or would allow her to deal with them more actively. She was a shy girl, and felt very uncomfortable about saying anything to anyone she did not know well. Therefore, she worked with the counsellor to develop defensive strategies.

While she found the avoiding strategies for strangers (see Box 3) useful, she needed to find a way of protecting herself from overt comments or stares. The counsellor taught her a technique known as *The Force-Field* (see Box 5). This is a type of visualization which can help people like Sophie withstand the comments of others. By using it, she is not acutely focused on who is saying things, but focuses rather on protecting herself from them. It also allows her to deal with comments which do get through to her, by seeing them as causing minor and reparable damage, not a global and total collapse.

Sophie though this technique sounded good fun. It appealed to her sense of humour, and she said she was prepared to try it. When she came back to say that she had done it and it had worked, she looked bright and cheerful. She felt more in control, and felt less worried about the potential threats posed by others. She felt she could deal with them, and this improved her self-esteem. It also helped her in her aims of being more independent as she now had more confidence in being able to go out into the world without her mother at her side.

Box 5: The Force-Field

Imagine that you are surrounded by an aura or some type of electro-magnetic field. It is projected from you, and covers your whole body. It is a colour, and can change colour depending on how you feel. Perhaps it is pink to start with.

Someone says something. They say 'Look at her face, it's awful'. The words come out of their mouth like an arrow or bullet. You hear them but they cannot penetrate you because they cannot get through your force-field. You may have to turn your force-field into a stronger colour to withstand these bullets, perhaps dark red. You concentrate on darkening the colour and strengthening the field. The words are deflected off your protective shield.

If you anticipate that something will be said, you can get your force-field ready. However, sometimes it happens out of the blue. The pink field may be strong enough, but perhaps it isn't and you are not prepared. The words get through. However, they do not cause a major explosion that affects all of you, they just cause a little damage and you draw your force-field in to repair it.

Julie. Following a traumatic and major disfiguring injury, the individual experiences social responses which will be radically different to those experienced before the injury. Sometimes the helper needs to provide very specific assistance in helping the person identify and understand these changed reactions and learn new social skills to deal with them. Julie had this problem following her burn injury.

The social worker spent time with Julie going out into a variety of places and helping her develop and practise the revised social skills she would need to deal with the reactions of other people and to manage social interactions. The first such sessions were spent in the local burger restaurant. As they walked down the street to the restaurant, they were both aware that people walking by were staring at Julie. The social worker acknowledged this for Julie, and said that they would deal with it later. He did not want Julie to feel isolated in the awareness of other people, but he also wanted the time to work through ways of dealing with this effectively.

When they walked into the restaurant, they walked up to the counter to place their order. The assistant glanced at Julie, looked away rapidly and spoke to the social worker. Although Julie spoke to the server, the server looked and replied to the social worker. She was clearly uncomfortable and fumbled with the order, wanting to get it over with as soon as possible. She did not smile.

They sat down to eat their burgers. The social worker asked Julie to describe what had just happened, and how that made her feel; he wanted Julie to acknowledge her own feelings, and to try to understand the feelings of the other person. Julie was very aware of the response of the server and felt upset and angry. He then asked her what she thought the server was thinking. Julie felt that the server was disgusted by her appearance. The social worker then asked Julie to consider whether there was anything she could do to improve the situation. Julie could only imagine avoiding it. He suggested that the server might not be disgusted, but might be anxious and not know how to respond, and perhaps Julie could help her with this. He suggested that Julie try to engage her by smiling at her when she looked at her. Julie was doubtful but said that she would try. She went up to order some drinks and smiled at the server. The server smiled back, and the ice was broken. Julie felt better and so did the server.

In this situation, Julie learned that if she kept an open mind about the responses of others, and assumed that they did not know what to do, she could control the situation because *she* knew what to do. This encouraged her to feel less helpless.

On another day, they went to the local market. Julie was stared at by people all the time, and she started keeping her head down to try to hide her face. They went for a cup of tea and discussed tactics. The strategy that had worked well in a one-to-one situation with a stranger was inappropriate here.

Julie had two main options. She could either hide her face or learn to ignore the stares. She agreed that she could not easily hide her face, but asked how she could ignore the staring when it was so intrusive. The social worker again asked her to interpret the responses of others. He asked her if she would have stared at a face that had been burnt before her accident. She said that she might have done, and when asked why, said because it looked so odd. She also felt people might be repulsed by her. However, the social worker suggested that if that was the case, then they would not stare but would look away. They decided to go for the first theory, that people were curious. It was important for Julie that the staring of others was not seen as too hostile an activity. It would have been hard for her to cope with too much overt and generalized hostility.

Together they agreed to try various ways of coping. Julie practised and used the way of unfocusing her eyes as described in Box 3.

Although this did allow her to feel some protection, she had a tendency to bump into people and hard objects, so it was not the most successful way of being inconspicuous! She eventually found the Force-Field technique (see Box 5) the most useful. She did not have to use it at its most intense as there were very few comments, but she did keep up a general level of protection which worked for her, and the stares did not penetrate her protective shield.

Although there were very few comments, when they happened they were very hurtful. They were either framed as questions, 'Whatever did you do to your face?', or as comments, 'Yuk, look at that'. Julie did not know what to say when the question was asked and did not want to talk about the fire as she found it so upsetting. She became very distressed when cruel comments were made. Talking with Julie, it was decided that when anyone asked her about her face, if she felt comfortable, she would say she had been in a fire. When she did not want to talk about it, she would reply 'Thank you for asking, but I'd rather not talk about it'. They practised this together in the room where she met with the social worker. He took the role of a stranger and asked her about her face. She tried out different ways of replying to this until she was able to find a way that felt right for her. At times he had to prompt her by taking her role and allowing her to take the role of the stranger. This encouraged her to consider things from the stranger's point of view, which helped her to feel less threatened by the stranger. It also allowed him to model for her how she could reply to others. The social worker was able to do this in a sensitive way which was responsive to Julie's needs because of the empathetic quality of their relation-ship – he understood that she needed help without feeling she was being dominated or controlled. The mutual trust enabled her to feel safe to role-play with him without feeling foolish or unsure of herself.

As for cruel comments, Julie decided that she would use her force-field more intently. There seemed no way of replying that she felt able to handle, and she did not want to provoke further aggression. She described fantasies of hitting the people who made such comments, and hurting them, and shared these with the social worker. They decided that as an outlet for her feelings of distress and aggression towards them, she would use a visualization of overcoming them behind her protective force-field. However, after she had done this a few times, she found that she could not be bothered as her sense that they had not hurt her made her feel superior, and therefore she did not feel threatened. Occasionally it did not work, and she became distressed, but the social worker encouraged her to learn from this, and to accept that she could not always be in control, but that she would recover and carry on.

Matthew. For children with a visible disfigurement, the school playground can be a difficult place. Young children may find it too difficult to handle the situation themselves and need more structured help from others. It might be appropriate to help them to express their feelings about this in order to understand the problem, and then to work through the teacher and the school.

The Special Needs teacher who was helping Matthew spent time with him encouraging him to express his feelings. He enjoyed doing the drawings and paintings, and together they talked through what he was saying in his pictures. It became clear that he envied his younger brother who did not have a cleft, and wished his face was like his brother's. He expressed his sadness that his face had not changed after surgery. Children at about the age of seven to eight years old with a facial anomaly tend to go through a grieving response, which is often compounded by the responses of other children. It was natural that Matthew should have negative feelings about his cleft as it was proving a problem for him at that time. He had hoped that surgery would eradicate the problem, illustrating the importance of ensuring that children understand the likely outcome of surgery.

When Matthew had expressed these feelings, he began to be happier and more like his old self. Before he returned to school, the Special Needs teacher talked with his class teacher and explained the situation. His own teacher then told the class that Matthew was coming back on Monday after his operation, and told them what he had had done. Thus, without revealing his vulnerability to the class, she prepared them for the lack of change. Matthew was pleased that she had done this, and felt more confident returning. The teacher also decided that she would use the opportunity to do some work with the class on bullying, and on encouraging kindness between them. This was done when Matthew was back, without any reference to him. The way schools can help deal with bullying has been described in a useful book by Olweus (1993). Strategies include:

measures at the school level:	– holding a day conference on the subject
	– better supervision of children away from lessons
	– a contact member of staff for victims
	– close contact between home and school
	– parent and teacher groups

measures at the class level: – class rules about bullying
                                         – the praising of positive behaviour
                                         – consistent sanctions for those who
                                                  bully
                                         – the use of co-operative learning

Matthew was soon happily settled in, and was not called names by the children in his class. He still had to endure occasional names from others, but the support and love of his family, his own resilient personality and the social support and acceptance by his friends and classmates all helped him.

Andrew and Tracy. Difficulties in social encounters can affect the parents as well as the child, and when the child is small, it can be more of a problem for the parents than for the child. Anxiety about letting others see their baby and handling their reactions can sometimes cause parents to avoid taking their baby out. For Andrew and Tracy, parents of young Jonathan, taking him out was very difficult, and the health visitor discussed this with them. Tracy said that she found herself watching people's faces in case they responded to her son critically. If she saw them staring, she would go up and shout at them to make them feel bad. However, if someone came up and asked what was the matter with his face, she could answer quite calmly that it was a birthmark. The health visitor asked her how that made her feel. She said that she felt better when she had explained calmly, and preferred that people ask. However, she found it difficult to control her anger when people stared.

The health visitor encouraged Tracy to consider why she thought they were staring. She had been very affected by the few people who had asked her what she had done to his face, or what he had done, and assumed that they were staring because they were critical. The health visitor then asked Andrew what he thought about this. He told how he had been in a hospital waiting-room with Jonathan and had seen a man with a port-wine stain, and had found himself staring. He said he had felt guilty about it once he realized what he was doing, and this helped them to recognize that staring was often to do with curiosity and making sense of things.

The health visitor suggested to them that Jonathan needed to learn how to deal with people himself, and that children learned by example. Therefore, it was important that they should find ways of working out how to deal with the responses of others that would be of benefit to him. They agreed that they did not want him to get into fights about it.

They also accepted that they did not always respond well; getting 'worked up' did little to increase people's understanding about the condition, which would help Jonathan. This discussion helped the parents to understand their own behaviour, and encouraged them to put Jonathan's needs before their own. It also helped them to formulate the goal that they wanted to enable Jonathan to deal with other people, and that this could partly be achieved through example.

Coping with Disruption to Normal Daily Life

A potential problem for those who have experienced a traumatic disfiguring injury is disruption to normal daily life, such as work and school. They are likely to have had to spend time in hospital and at home, and they are then faced with the need to resume their normal activities with an altered appearance.

Re-entry to school

The social world of school can be very difficult for children who have had a major disfiguring injury. They may have been away from school for some time, and have lost contact with their friends and classmates. They return looking different. This re-entry needs careful management in order to minimize these social problems.

Julie. Julie was away from school for many months following her burn injury. Before she was fit enough to return to school, Julie needed to keep up with her education so that she would not fall too far behind her class-mates. The social worker got in touch with the local education authority to inquire about home teaching. Julie was assessed and allocated a home teacher who spent three hours each day with her. The teacher liaised with the school and obtained work for Julie to do. The teacher also provided daily contact for her, and became a source of support.

It was the teacher who persuaded Julie to let a few of her friends visit, and they brought work from school to her. Julie wanted only her two closest friends to come, and her form teacher suggested that she call by with them to talk with Julie and see how she was getting on. Although Julie had tolerated being seen by professionals who had not known her before the fire, she was very apprehensive about the responses of her friends. However, the teacher had already seen Julie in hospital and was able to prepare her friends, so that they were not obviously shocked when they saw her. The friends started calling by regularly with work for Julie and the appearance of her face soon became familiar to them.

This regular informal contact with her close friends helped Julie realize that people could talk to her and accept her. This gave her some confidence to start thinking about the next stage, her return to school.

As Julie recovered, the education authority expected that she would return to school. This was planned by Julie, the social worker, the home tutor, the head of year at the school and Julie's family, and it was agreed that it would be a gradual return. However, Julie had still not been able to go out and about, and walking into school that first day was a major obstacle for her.

The social worker helped Julie prepare for this. He borrowed a video camera and took it to Julie's home, so that she could record a message for her friends on videotape. The social worker then took the tape into school and showed it to the staff, explaining Julie's physical treatment and future plans. Afterwards he led a discussion about the meaning of disfigurement, and ways of helping Julie and the other children to deal with it within school. The tape was then shown at a special school assembly, with some explanation about the extent of the burns and what further treatment was likely to be carried out. This process allowed the children to look and be shocked and upset, and to ask questions before Julie was there. People often want to stare at a face with disfigurement, and it is better to stare at a recorded image. The teachers then worked with their individual classes, asking the children to imagine how Julie would feel when she returned, and using that as a basis for preparing them to be supportive of her. Thus the situation was used to guide the children towards a greater understanding of the needs of people with disfigurement.

Julie was aware that this was happening. She did not want to be there, and was nervous about how people would respond, but her friends were able to tell her that people had been very kind about it and hoped she would come back soon. She also received many cards and messages from other teachers and children saying the same thing, so she knew that they knew how she looked, but had accepted her.

She returned to school for the first time the following week. The children had been advised not to make too much fuss, but to greet her if they knew her, and otherwise to get on with their own activities. She gradually increased her time at school, and soon settled back in happily. This was interrupted by further surgery, but the school developed a pattern of getting work to her.

This process helped Julie to make the transition to school. It was also helpful to the school, as it gave staff the opportunity to use this experience to increase the other children's awareness and empathy. Julie's mother was not part of this, although she was pleased it was happening, but she felt that she was still struggling with her own feelings and was not ready to help others.

Returning to work

Many adults are injured in the work-place. If they are able to resume their previous employment, then they have to return to the environment in which the accident took place. The sight of the work-place and the machinery may trigger post-traumatic symptoms, such as heightened anxiety, intrusive flashbacks and disturbing nightmares. Some people need help in overcoming these experiences in order to get back to work.

John. John had problems returning to work following his hand injury. The Occupational Therapist working with him knew that the earlier this is tackled, the more likely it is to be successful. Postponing the return would have increased a sense of foreboding, and allowed mental pictures of the incident and the machinery to become overwhelming. A long delay would also have created practical problems, as John had financial problems and was worried that the firm would not keep the job open for him. The OT's approach was to help him gradually get used to the environment of work once more. Any contact with the scene of his accident caused John anxiety, so the OT ensured that he learned relaxation techniques to help him cope with this before he started to return to work. These techniques have already been described (see page 85).

The OT saw John on a daily basis, and started the process of gradual exposure to the stimulus (the work situation) by encouraging him to visualize the machinery and to describe it in words. As John thought about the machinery, he started to feel sweaty and his heart pounded. The OT was watching him closely and observed his distress. He reminded him of the relaxation techniques he had learned to help control the physical symptoms of anxiety. With the help of these techniques, John found that he was able to talk about the machinery more easily, and could describe it in detail. The more he was able to talk about it, the easier he found it to remember.

After three days of this, John went on a visit to the factory with the OT for support and looked at the machinery for the first time. As he approached the scene of the accident he felt very anxious, but the OT reminded him to keep his breathing steady and to relax his body. He stayed for a while until he could feel these symptoms subsiding. The following day, he went into work and started working on the machinery. He was encouraged to consider ways of controlling its safety, as he was hyper-alert, jumping whenever he heard a sudden sound from the machine. He continued to use relaxation techniques to allow him to cope, and also decided that he would talk to his work-mates about his jumpiness, as he had found people sympathetic in other situations. They were encouraging, and made jokes about it, which he appreciated, as they helped defuse the situation and reduce his tension. He soon found that he could work at the machine without too much difficulty, although he remained very alert to the workings of it, and was very careful what he did. He was relieved to find that he could work again, and financial pressures eased.

Coping with body image problems

People who are disfigured may feel self-conscious about their disfigurement. This can be expressed as an intense awareness of the disfigurement which develops into a preoccupation affecting emotions and social behaviour. Many of the problems with social encounters previously described are profoundly affected by the individual's self-consciousness, and hostile reactions from others can induce or intensify feelings of self-consciousness. Thus the two areas of difficulty are closely linked, and it is likely that helping people with social encounters will reduce their sense of self-consciousness and heightened visibility to others.

John. John was very self-conscious about the appearance of his hand following the injury to it, and the Occupational Therapist worked with him on this problem (see Box 6 for a summary of the principles of desensitization). At the beginning of the sessions, the OT asked John to record subjectively on a scale of 0 to 10 the extent of his concern about his hand with different people. 0 was the 'most easy' and 10 was the 'most difficult' he could imagine. Thus he found that he scored 3 for letting the surgeon and OT see it, 7 for seeing it himself, 8 for his girlfriend and 10 for everyone else. This was a useful baseline against which to record progress.

The OT approached this problem in terms of helping John to get used to the appearance of his hand, and because John felt that he could trust the OT not to manipulate or control him, he was able to work with him on this. The OT had also shown that he accepted the appearance of John's hand by touching it freely when treating it, and by being able to look at it easily. This relaxed and accepting approach signalled to John that he did not need to feel self-conscious about it in that setting.

Box 6: Principles of desensitization

- Anxiety may be aroused by sensory triggers associated with the feared situation; thus, the smell of the operating theatre may act as a trigger which arouses feelings of anxiety and panic because it reminds the person of the feared situation, the operation itself.
- Gradual exposure to the trigger will reduce those feelings of anxiety and help the individual to feel more in control of his or her reactions and behaviour.
- The individual is more likely to tolerate this exposure to the trigger if it is accompanied by ways of controlling the physical symptoms of anxiety, such as controlled breathing.
- By reducing the feelings of anxiety provoked by the triggers, the individual is more able to face the feared situation and cope with it.

The OT asked John to show him the hand, to touch it himself and to talk about how it had changed. When John became upset and looked away, the OT was reassuring, acknowledging John's difficulty but encouraging him to look back at it. The more they talked about the hand, the more John was able to look at it, and he agreed that he would not cover it when on his own at home. Once he had recognized that he was hiding it from himself, he was able to make progress. After a few weeks, he recorded that he would now score 3 for himself seeing it, and 5 for his girlfriend, who had helped him at home, and between 8 and 9 for everyone else. Thus John could see progress, and became encouraged by the feeling that he was regaining control.

He then identified for himself situations when other people might see his hand, but which would not be too difficult to deal with, such as walking down the street or going shopping. In these situations he was dealing with strangers, and so did not find it too difficult. Whenever he needed to, he used his relaxation techniques. The greatest stumbling block for him was social situations with acquaintances; he still found he was uncomfortable in pubs when people saw his hand, and this remained at a difficulty score of about 7.

The OT then moved on to the use of a *script* – that is, what he wanted to say and how he wanted to say it. The script was generated by discussing with John what he thought other people were thinking about his hand. During this discussion, it became clear that he believed that others would think he was deformed and ugly. The OT then asked John what he thought they would say and how he would like to reply. At first he only suggested hostile remarks, but with encouragement was able to suggest some questions that might be based on curiosity. He told the OT how he would like to reply to all these remarks and the OT wrote this all down. The OT helped him practise these replies by taking the role of the other person. They also considered what John would say to those who stared but said nothing.

When John did go out without covering his hand, he found that people either stared or asked him in an interested way about his hand. There were no hostile remarks. Because of what he had practised with the OT, he was able to mention that he had had an accident at work, and found that people took this very easily, rapidly losing interest in his hand. Thus John could test the reality of his beliefs about his hand and its effect on others, and found their responses reassuring. He also found that many other people had experienced hand injuries, which decreased his feelings of isolation. He soon began to resume his normal relationships with other people, and found he could joke about his hand.

Sophie. Sophie found that as she grew more confident in social encounters, she could talk more freely to the school counsellor about her feelings of self-consciousness and distress about her face. In particular, she became very upset one day and cried about her face. She felt that it wasn't fair. The counsellor supported this and encouraged her to express her feelings, thus supporting her in her feelings of loss and bereavement. She made no attempt to find solutions, as she recognized that there was no easy solution to this, and that Sophie needed to be able to express her feelings without anyone trying to minimize or change them. This calm and supportive listening allowed Sophie to move through the grieving process and no longer deny the reality of her face. She was then able to allow herself to accept that surgery would do no magic, and it was this realization that was part of her distress.

Julie. Julie had great difficulty in coming to terms with her altered appearance. At first, she avoided looking at herself, followed by a stage of being pre-occupied with her appearance. This was not a problem which could be solved easily, and the social worker spent time with Julie encouraging her to talk about how she felt, rather than trying to change her feelings or minimize their importance. He let her express all her anger and distress by listening in a calm and caring way, and by reflecting back where necessary to encourage Julie to talk.

Throughout this work, Julie's social worker showed that he cared about her, but without being upset himself. He provided a safe 'holding' relationship which allowed her to talk through her sorrow and sense of loss. However, it was difficult work as Julie became very distressed at times and went through a phase of saying she wished that she had died in the fire. He found that Julie's anguish weighed on his mind, and that he was thinking about her at home and feeling unhappy himself. He began to put off seeing Julie, because it was becoming too great a burden. He arranged to talk about this with his supervisor at their next session; he was tempted to talk to his wife about it, but knew that this would be a breach of confidentiality, and would also bring Julie's problems into his home situation. His supervisor provided valuable support in helping him deal with his distress and feelings of helplessness at being unable to 'solve' the terrible physical and emotional damage caused by the burns. The helper in this situation often needs help, and this will be discussed in the final chapter of this book.

Sexual identity. For some people with a visible disfigurement, concern about their body image has an impact on their sexual identity and their sexual relationships with others. This is particularly true for the growing adolescent who is entering the world of sexual activity.

As Julie grew up, she became more aware of boys, and saw that her friends were beginning to go out with them. She remained socially quite reclusive, and did not want to go to nightclubs where she felt she might be rejected. She became moody and irritable and her mother arranged for her to see the social worker again. He met with her and referred her to a female colleague, which seemed more appropriate at this stage.

She encouraged Julie to talk about how she felt, and Julie needed this opportunity to talk about her perception that her damaged body was sexually unattractive. This was not a problem that could be solved: the reality was that most boys would not be attracted to Julie. The helper listened to her in a supportive way, allowing her to explore her feelings in a safe environment and making no effort to modify her thoughts or feelings. However, the more Julie talked, the more angry and unhappy she became. In this situation, listening skills were not enough; the more the problem was examined, the greater it seemed to become.

The helper then moved to a more problem-solving approach. They set the aim of Julie having a more active social life and mixing with both boys and girls. This was a realistic aim, and together they worked out ways that Julie might meet boys in a more relaxed way. She started going to the local Youth Club, and became involved in a voluntary scheme to help disabled children. She was asked out by someone also working in that scheme, with whom she eventually developed a sexual relationship, although she found it hard to allow him to see or touch her breasts. She thought he would be disgusted by them, but he had been aware of her burns when he asked her out, and had no difficulty seeing or touching her. Julie was fortunate that the first sexual relationship she had was so supportive, and although the relationship did not last, it allowed her to get over an important and difficult hurdle.

Making Decisions about Treatment

Those with disfigurement may be offered treatment to improve their appearance and perhaps also to improve the function of their limbs or facial movements. Thus a person with burns to the neck may be offered surgery to improve the appearance of his or her neck which will also release the tight skin and allow more movement. However, it is not always easy to decide about surgery; the person may be anxious about the operation and its outcome, there may be unresolved emotional issues influencing decisions, or it may be felt that further surgery is too disruptive. The offer of reconstruction can stir up many painful feelings. By suggesting improvements that could be made, there is an implication that the way the individual looks now is somehow unacceptable. In addition, the possible outcome will have to be weighed up against all the discomfort and inconvenience of surgery, and the concern that the person may not be able to cope with their changed appearance. Those with disfigurement can be helped to reach decisions which are stable and satisfactory, whether they chose to proceed or not to proceed with treatment.

Maria. Maria had to decide whether to go ahead with surgery to improve her hemi-facial palsy. The outcome was uncertain and the surgery was major. She could not contemplate making this decision until she had been able to talk through her concerns and work with the liaison nurse to deal with her social and emotional problems. They set time aside to deal with this specific issue. The nurse asked her to describe all her concerns about surgery; these included fear of the anaesthetic, concern about her final appearance, and worries about potential scarring. The nurse wrote these down and encouraged Maria to separate short-term issues such as the operation itself from long-term issues such as final technical outcome.

Maria then looked at her current difficulties and concerns, and talked through whether they would be helped by any improvement in appearance. She had begun to feel more in control of her life as she grew more confident in her ability to relate to other people, thus recognizing that she did not **need** surgery in order to bring about change or to be acceptable to herself. However, she was also able to understand that the more disfigured she looked to others, the more she had to work at coping. She felt that an improvement in her appearance would help this process, and in particular, an improvement in her smile would be useful to her. She was then able to discuss specific technical issues with the surgeon without distress.

Sophie. Sophie also had to make decisions about surgery. Having worked through feelings of loss and adjustment, Sophie was then ready to go back to the surgeon's out-patient clinic to discuss having surgery to improve her face. She prepared for this with the counsellor by taking with her a list of specific questions she wanted to be answered. She also gave some thought to what it was about her face she wanted to change, and decided that she would like her nose to be improved in its shape, and would also find out what else could be done. She was clear about her priorities, but prepared to listen to the surgeon's advice.

The surgeon suggested to Sophie that he could improve the shape of her nose, and explained clearly what changes he could bring about. She felt happy to go ahead with that. He then said that he could move her jaw to improve the alignment and profile of her face, and that he could also do some work on her skull to improve her forehead. She said little at this point, and went away to think about it. When she next met the school counsellor, she told her what he had said and became tearful as she talked. The counsellor listened carefully. She recognized from Sophie's reactions that the offer of surgery had been very threatening to her. However, Sophie was uncommunicative about her real feelings about it and the counsellor decided to force the issue by suggesting that surgery was clearly a good idea as it would improve her appearance, and also reminded her that she wanted to look better. The counsellor moved out of her non-judgemental and non-directive role in order to confront and to understand Sophie's reactions. Sophie became angry with her, saying that she had tried hard to come to terms with the way she looked, and whilst it seemed reasonable to improve her nose, she felt that other surgery was a more fundamental assault on her rather fragile self-acceptance. She said that despite her own efforts to accept herself, her face was still fundamentally unacceptable to other people. By offering this surgery, the surgeon had underlined this for her. At this point, the surgeon and the counsellor were merged in Sophie's mind, and both seemed to be pushing her towards surgery. Because she had gained some self-confidence in herself, she was now able to say this.

The decision about surgery triggered a crisis for Sophie, and revealed hidden feelings about herself, that she was 'abnormal' because of her craniofacial condition. The counsellor allowed the anger to be expressed without reacting back in an angry way. She did not take Sophie's reactions personally, and recognized that although the anger was directed at her, she was not the reason for it, she had just been instrumental in releasing it. Sophie was able to say to her what she had wanted to say to the surgeon. Once she had said this, she felt calmer and more in control of events, and was able to start thinking clearly about whether she should have surgery.

Sophie came more happily to the next session. She felt better for having revealed her deepest concerns in a warm and supportive atmosphere, and was able to talk about what she had said. Together they discussed feelings of being different, and how that was not the same as being unacceptable. Sophie decided that she could live with the way she looked, but that any improvement would be a bonus to her as it would ease the work of managing new interactions. Because she felt confident that she could now do this, she recognized that it was not weakness on her part to have surgery. However, she did have some anxiety about her ability to cope with her changed post-surgical appearance, although admittedly this was an anxiety mixed with excited anticipation.

Sophie decided to go ahead with the surgery suggested by the surgeon. This was extensive and she had three major operations. She coped well with the surgery itself, although she was rather appalled by how swollen and disfigured she looked in the early days after craniofacial surgery. As time went by, the swelling settled and she went back to see the surgeon, who was delighted with the result. Her friends and family were also very pleased, and everyone agreed that it was a great improvement.

Sophie took time to adjust to her changed appearance. She had lived all her life looking the way she had looked, and she had gone through a difficult period of adjustment in order to accept herself in adolescence. She found that she needed to spend a lot of time studying her face in the mirror, but she felt rather ashamed of this, as she felt she was becoming vain. The counsellor reassured her that she was going through a period of further adjustment, and that she needed to allow herself this time. Sophie found that strangers reacted to her differently, and she wanted to talk about that. She realized that she was not noticed so much, and had become less conspicuous to others. However, friends reacted to her in the same way, and that helped to reassure her that although her appearance had changed, the person she was had not changed.

Coping with the Process of Treatment

Sometimes decisions about treatment can be profoundly affected by a fear of the actual treatment process. Treatment for burns can be very painful, and there are often many operations to go through, particularly for a child whose skin cannot grow properly because of the tight constriction caused by the burn scarring.

Julie. Julie had to deal with a seemingly endless round of hospital visits and surgical treatment. Although hospital became a familiar place to her, she did not like going down to theatre. She had become phobic about needles, and the smell of the operating theatre also triggered panic. The hospital staff assumed that because she had had a lot of treatment, she would get used to it. However, as with many others in her situation, she associated it with pain and discomfort. She also felt out of control and distressed when she went to theatre, a reflection of her feelings that life had gone out of control.

Although the doctors and nurses talked to her, she did not always understand what they were saying. Julie felt that they used too much medical jargon, and assumed that she was familiar with the issues. However, over the years as she grew up her ability to process information was changing, and she needed to have things explained at a level she understood. She discussed this with the social worker, who encouraged her to speak out about this in clinic and to say if she did not understand. Together they identified when this would be appropriate and what would be the best way of doing it. They wrote down the usual sequence of events in clinic and the details of a visit she remembered where the communication had been unsatisfactory. Julie said what she had wanted to ask and was helped by the warm and encouraging approach of the social worker to find a way of framing the questions she wanted to ask. Because she was often overwhelmed by all the people in clinic, she decided that she would prefer to write her questions down. They then looked at the pattern of a clinic visit and decided that it would be best to ask straight away when she went in, before the discussion became technical. In this situation it could have been tempting for the social worker to take over and do the asking for Julie, or suggest that her mother did this. However, this would not have enabled Julie to feel competent and in control of events.

During the course of her treatment, Julie had to undergo many operations and procedures which were stressful for her. She began to anticipate the discomfort and pain and grew increasingly anxious. However, she knew that the treatment would improve her appearance and help her to cope with her disfigurement so it was important that she was helped to cope with this treatment.

The burns unit sister prepared Julie for surgery. She taught Julie the relaxation techniques described earlier, and in particular taught her to control her breathing. She then suggested that when Julie saw that she was going to have an injection, or any other treatment that was difficult for her, she do three things.

1. *Look away*: this distracted Julie and ensured that the sight of the needle did not trigger a phobic response. The sister encouraged Julie to look at her and away from the process of treatment. By holding her attention in this way, she was able to talk her through the other ways of coping with treatment.

2. *Steady her breathing and consciously relax her body*: this reduces the physical symptoms of anxiety. The sister used the same breathing techniques and method of physical relaxation described and talked Julie through it as she prepared for treatment. She was able to reinforce this whenever she saw that Julie's breathing was getting more rapid and her body was tensing.

3. *Focus her mind on something pleasant as a form of visualization:* this was another means of distraction. Before she went for treatment, they practised this together, and Julie described a scene from a film she liked where the woman in the film is given a credit card to buy all the clothes she wants from expensive shops. This was to be her visualization. The sister was then able to remind her of it when she became distressed.

The sister was aware that the theatre smell remained a trigger for anxiety. She took Julie down one evening before surgery when there was no one there apart from a nurse who showed them round. They changed into the blue clothes worn by theatre staff. Julie was at first repelled by the smell, but the sister suggested that she do her relaxation breathing and concentrate on breathing in the smell and breathing it out again – in other words, showing her that she could get rid of it. Julie soon realized that she had grown accustomed to it and could no longer smell it. She then was able to explore the theatre, seeing in more detail the things she had only seen out of the corner of her eye, such as the black oxygen cylinders. She talked with the theatre nurse and discovered that they played music she liked during the operation as background noise. All this helped Julie to perceive the operating theatre as somewhere people worked, and she began to feel at ease there.

The next day, when she went down to theatre, she used her breathing control and visualization techniques. She found that the place was now more familiar, and she did not feel upset, just slightly apprehensive.

Reaching a Conclusion about Further Treatment

There came a point when Julie felt that she did not want any more surgery. The surgeon could go on revising areas, but this became a problem for Julie, as it meant that she had to keep dealing with physical treatment and she missed schooling and social activities with friends. It also encouraged a belief that there would be a solution to the physical problems. In particular, it postponed the task of coming to terms with her appearance – the task of final re-integration of her altered body image. It is often easier to continue treatment as this postpones this task of adjustment. Julie also felt that she might be letting down her kindly and enthusiastic surgeon. However, when she was 16 she decided that she would have no further surgery for the foreseeable future.

Because she had been encouraged by the social worker to speak out in clinic, and had grown confident in her ability to do so, she was able to say this to the surgeon. The help she had received over the years since the fire had allowed her to express her distress away from the clinic, and so she could speak calmly in clinic. The surgeon accepted her decision, and said that she could always come back in the future if she changed her mind. This was important to her, as it indicated that doors had not been closed and that she had not upset those who had cared for her. Julie was thus able to feel that she had handled the situation well.

Coping Without Treatment

Some people need help in coming to terms with the fact that there is no physical treatment available for their condition. This can be particularly hard for parents whose children have a disfigurement and who desperately want to improve their child's appearance.

Andrew and Tracy. Jonathan's parents had been told by more than one expert that the haemiangioma would look better as time went by, and that no treatment should be considered before their son was seven years old. Their reaction to this was one of anger, as they felt that they were being denied treatment. The health visitor worked with them to help them understand their own reactions and to let go of their hopes for immediate treatment. She began this by looking with them at the reality of the situation. Although they felt that there had been no improvement, she found early clinical pictures of Jonathan which showed that the haemiangioma was improving. This confirmed what they had been told. She encouraged each of them to say what they had wanted from treatment, asking them to list what they would have gained from any intervention, and what they would have lost. She reminded them of the medical information they had received, so that they realized that they might have gained a slight improvement but Jonathan would have had facial scarring from the surgery. By waiting, there was a possibility that he would need no treatment, thus avoiding any scarring. The health visitor helped Andrew and Tracy to face the reality of the situation in a calm and straightforward way, and to clearly separate medical issues from other issues.

This enabled her to move on to discuss with them why they had been so upset. She did this by suggesting to each of them that they complete the sentence 'I was upset because. . .'. Tracy was able to say that she was upset because she found it hard to take Jonathan out and thought surgery would solve this problem for her. Andrew said that he was upset because he felt that the doctors were withholding treatment. The health visitor was able to challenge this based on their earlier discussion. At this point Andrew became angry again, this time directing his anger at the health visitor. She felt this was unfair and became angry with him in response. He left, and she realized that she had made the mistake of working within Andrew's tightly-defined agenda, which was physical treatment. She had been unable to maintain non-judgemental acceptance because she had taken his reactions personally by identifying with the professionals treating Jonathan. She discussed this with a colleague at work, who advised her to set up a further meeting with both parents.

At this next meeting, she was able to explain her reaction to Andrew, which helped him to say that he had over-reacted. She showed empathic understanding of this by her open and accepting manner, and her willingness to admit her own over-reaction allowed the relationship to become more equal. She suggested that they leave behind the issue of treatment and try to cope with the situation as it was. The time had come to find ways of coping with the difficulties they were experiencing. Re-framing the problem in a more positive and forward-looking way avoided any criticism.

Coping with Post-Traumatic Symptoms

Those who have been through a traumatic injury may be experiencing post-traumatic symptoms which can cause problems as described earlier. However, for many people, these are transitory problems and they can be helped through them.

John. John found that he was helped by working with the OT and that he was more able to look at his hand and let others see it. However, the post-traumatic symptoms remained, and he continued to be on a 'short fuse', particularly with his girlfriend; thus the relationship problem had merged with that of post-traumatic stress. The OT then looked with him at the continuing problems relating to this. The approach was two-fold.

1. *Normalizing the experience through reassurance and information.* John thought that his personality had changed forever because of his injury, and his post-traumatic symptoms made him feel that he was 'going mad' at times. He was reassured to learn that these symptoms were a normal response to his injury, and that in time, and with support, it was likely that they would lessen. Thus he learned that what seemed like permanent damage to his personality was actually a pattern of responses which were characteristic of post-traumatic stress. This was extremely important for him and reduced his levels of anxiety.

2. *Re-evaluation of changed beliefs.* John had developed a set of changed beliefs about himself and the world because of his injury, and it was only in discussion that these became clear. He no longer felt that the world was a safe place to be for him or those he loved, and he felt that he was no longer in control of his life. These beliefs are typical of people who have been through trauma, and can make the process of recovery difficult. It is a fundamental blow to a person's

psychological well-being. For some people, where levels of anxiety and depression inhibit normal functioning, specialist psychological intervention is carried out by an experienced psychologist or psychiatrist. However, for John, these feelings did not deeply affect his functioning, but did make him rather anxious.

The OT used open-ended questions to find out what was worrying him at that time. He asked John if there were any thoughts that were particularly troubling him. John said that he had become anxious when he was driving, so the OT asked him what thoughts worried him when he was driving. John said that he did not trust other drivers and thought he would be involved in a crash. Thus he was encouraged to describe what he felt were irrational and strange ideas, and was listened to in an accepting and uncritical way. The OT asked him to talk about his driving experiences in the past; encouraging John to look back to situations where he had been in control, thus challenging his belief that he could not control events. He also explained to John that these generalized feelings of anxiety were part of the natural responses to traumatic injury, and that his confidence would return in time.

By mutual agreement, the sessions were terminated when John was back at work full-time.

Coping with Adjustment to the Birth

The process of adjustment facing many parents who have a baby with a visible disfigurement has been described in Chapter 2.

Andrew and Tracy. For Andrew and Tracy, parents of Jonathan, help came a few years after he was born, but they were still having adjustment problems. It would have been more appropriate to have offered that help when Jonathan was born, and that might have enabled his parents to cope more easily. However, for these parents, the focus had been on the search for treatment. When they had been helped to accept that there was no treatment available, as described on p. 107, then they were ready to cope with their reactions to Jonathan's birth.

The health visitor encouraged them to talk about how they had reacted to Jonathan at birth and as the mark grew. She used the effective listening skills described in Chapter 3 to encourage them to talk, and accepted their negative feelings towards Jonathan without judgement. They both became upset talking about this. The health visitor recognized that it was important for Tracy to see that Andrew was also tearful. She had not realized that he had been as upset as she, and the health visitor left them with the suggestion that they talk this through together. Because she listened in an empathic and caring way, they felt their emotions were valid, and were able to relax a little. In particular, Andrew was able to lower his defences and show his feelings. Thus the health visitor helped unite these parents and facilitated communication between them. It was within this context that the health visitor explored Andrew and Tracy's responses to their son's facial anomaly. At the first session, she had encouraged them to express their emotions, and had facilitated a greater synchronicity between these emotions by helping each of them to recognize and respond to the feelings of the other.

The health visitor explored practical issues with Andrew and Tracy, such as the taking of photos. They had taken photos of Jonathan but very few, and did not display them. They now had a little girl, whose photos were all round the house. The health visitor discussed this with them, suggesting that Jonathan might eventually feel that his sister was more loved because her photos were on display. They felt that they could not tolerate having his photos on display, so it was suggested that they take some photos of both children together, minimizing his mark by the lighting or the angle of the shot. If these were displayed, it would begin the process of having photos of Jonathan for others to see. In this way the health visitor recognized Andrew and Tracy's difficulties, and helped them to find ways of achieving the aim of showing photos of their son without being confronted by the birthmark.

Another issue which had relevance in their adjustment to Jonathan was their attitude to further children. They discussed with the health visitor how they had felt about their second child. They knew that a haemiangioma did not appear at first, and was certainly not picked up on a scan, so they would have no way of anticipating it. However, this did not interfere with their plans for another child, although when she was born, they studied her very carefully. Their reactions to this showed that they did not view the haemiangioma as so serious that it would affect decisions about further children. Referring the parents to a genetic counsellor can be helpful as it enables them to consider what chance they had of having further children with the same condition.

The health visitor then spent time with Andrew and Tracy discussing how the whole situation had affected them as a couple. She asked them to describe the benefits as well as the problems, and this helped them to focus on ways in which they had drawn together rather than concentrating on any difficulties which had been generated. Andrew's reactions in an earlier session when he had shown his emotions had been very important to them as a couple. She was able to reflect this back to them, and also the way in which they had both been so involved in Jonathan's care.

At this point, the parents felt more ready to move the focus away from themselves and towards Jonathan. By working through the issues described, they had been able to resolve their own feelings and to recognize the importance of separating their own needs from those of Jonathan. They wanted to know how best to deal with Jonathan's questions. At bed-time a few weeks before, he had asked why he had the mark on his face and had said that he did not want to look like that and wanted it taken away. Tracy had been dreading the day when he would start to ask questions, but she handled it well. She quietly told him that it was a birthmark, that it was getting smaller but would take a long time to go, and that it could not be taken away. Tracy became tearful recounting this, but the health visitor reassured her that she had reacted to this in a way which would help him in the future. By praising Tracy's interaction with her son on this difficult issue, the health visitor encouraged her to feel more competent as a parent and thus more able to deal with difficulties in the future. Building parents' belief in their own parenting skills is an important aim of helping.

The health visitor also worked with them to help them understand what may have been behind Jonathan's question. She reminded them that Jonathan was only a small child, and the fact that he had recognized his haemiangioma and not wanted it was perfectly natural at this stage in his development. He did not show any particular signs of distress, and was merely asking a logical question and stating the obvious – he did not like it. Thus the health visitor helped by focusing on *Jonathan's* needs rather than on *their* needs. If Tracy had been tearful in front of Jonathan, or not able to give him a clear answer, then he might well have perceived her distress and thought that this mark was very serious as it upset his parents. His anxiety would have been aroused, and feelings of self-consciousness and shame might have begun.

Andrew and Tracy wondered what to do when Jonathan asked further questions. The health visitor encouraged them to build on what they had learned from his first question, and reflected back to them their recognition that a calm approach worked well. She then asked them to consider when he might ask, and how they could ensure that they were able to listen to him carefully and answer him in a helpful way. She encouraged them to develop skills of effective listening, and talked about how this could be achieved through a warm and understanding reaction and a non-judgemental approach, using open-ended questions to find out what he wanted to know. The temptation would be for parents to use rhetorical questions, such as 'You must be really upset, mustn't you?', to confirm their worst fears for their child. Thus the helper can pass on her knowledge about helping skills to give parents a greater sense of competence.

The health visitor suggested to them that if they were able to answer Jonathan's questions in a straightforward way, then he would be able to answer others' questions. Thus helping them to talk with him about his disfigurement was of importance for Jonathan in his social inter-actions. She explained that it was unlikely that he would become self-conscious about his birthmark before the age of about five or six, and the more he was able to talk about it and answer other people, the less impact it would have on him. He was a lively and outgoing little boy, and his parents were worried that it would affect his personality, but were reassured to know that it worked the other way – his personality would help him to be more resilient.

The help given by the health visitor in coping with Jonathan's own reactions was of importance in their adjustment to him as they were able to develop a sense of competent parenting, giving them the confidence to deal with any further problems as they arose.

Coping with the Reactions of Family and Friends

Although the helper generally becomes involved in helping the individual with the disfigurement, it can be that other family members also need help, and this needs to be identified. Sometimes it is appropriate for the helper to do this work, but sometimes he or she may need to call upon other agencies to help.

Maria's husband. Maria had identified difficulties in her relationship with her husband and asked the liaison nurse if she would talk with him. She preferred not to be present for this session. Her husband talked with the nurse about how Maria had changed over the years, saying that it was her changed behaviour and not her changed appear-ance that he found difficult. The nurse felt it was appropriate to refer on to another agency specializing in couple counselling. There are times when referring on is an important way of helping. Such a referral should take place when:

a) *the problem is outside the helper's competence.* In this case, the nurse had never worked with couples and did not feel that she understood how best to help them.

b) *the problem is wider than the immediate issue.* It was clear that there were long-standing problems between Maria and her husband, only some of which related to the disfigurement.

c) *there would be a conflict of loyalties.* The helper felt that she had developed a good helping relationship with Maria, and this could be threatened if she also worked with her husband.

Decisions about appropriate referral agencies are based on the specific needs of the situation. The agencies of choice should always be those which operate within the public sector, such as educational psychology or social services, as by referring to such agencies, the helper can be sure that there are regulated standards of care. Other bona fide agencies such as RELATE are also well-regulated. The issue of referral is discussed further in the final chapter.

Sophie's parents. Sophie had been worried about her parents' distress, and had been relieved to know that they would be offered help. However, because Sophie's counsellor worked within the school and because of the issue of confidentiality, it was felt more appropriate that they should see someone else for this help. They went to talk with their family doctor who was very supportive. He asked them to talk about how they had felt when Sophie was born, and encouraged them to describe their emotional reactions at the time. Because Sophie's mother wept when talking about this, it was clear to the GP that there were unresolved adjustment problems and that she needed particular help to deal with this. She started to talk about difficulties in her own childhood, and the GP recognized that she needed time and skilled help. He referred her to the psychotherapist at the local hospital for more specialist intervention to help her to explore her emotional state and her long-standing problems.

Julie's mother. Julie's mother and sister had also been profoundly affected by her injury. In particular, Julie's mother felt a terrible burden of guilt and responsibility, a common reaction in parents. She found that when she went out with Julie, she was hyper-vigilant, watching the faces of other people and looking out for any adverse reaction. She was displacing a lot of her own anger and guilt on to others. On several occasions she shouted at people who were pointing, leaving her feeling tense and exhausted.

The social worker arranged for the counsellor from the GP's practice to work with Julie's mother. She spent time allowing her to express her feelings and talk through her guilt and distress. The most important help that Julie's mother could receive at this time was to feel that she was understood and accepted despite her feelings of guilt; once she received that help, she was more able to help Julie. Because she was experiencing the reactions of others together with her daughter, she needed help in coping with social encounters, so she was taught relaxation skills to ease her hyper-vigilance, and also the ways of ignoring others as described in Maria's section. Thus she learned to walk down the street without seeing other people's responses, and was able to concentrate on Julie.

Julie's sister. The social worker also saw Julie's sister for some sessions, as she was having problems at school. She was disturbed by what had happened, and felt guilty because she had gone out on the evening of the fire and because Julie was burned and she had not been burned. She needed help at different levels. The first type of help she needed was that of information – she had not been included in visits to clinic and discussions about treatment, and thus felt she did not know what was happening. The social worker talked with her and explained clearly what had happened to Julie, the treatment that was planned and why Julie needed that treatment. She also encouraged Julie and her mother to include the sister in their visits to hospital and in their discussions.

The social worker recognized the trauma that Julie's sister had experienced and gave her the opportunity to talk about this. She was young and found it hard to express her feelings in words, so the social worker took her to a playroom in the local community clinic where they could spend time together without interruption. Julie's sister used toys to re-enact the events of the fire and also played with the hospital set. She did this many times until she gradually began to lose interest and moved on to play in a different way. She was using play as a means of making sense of what had happened.

With both Julie's sister and mother, the helper worked to involve them in Julie's care as a way of allowing her to build support within the family structure rather than rely on long-term professional help. However, both needed individual help before they could do this.

Evaluating Outcome and Drawing the Process to a Conclusion

The final part of the helping process involves a transition away from the helping relationship. Throughout the process, the helper should have worked with the individual to evaluate progress. The evaluation of outcome is a joint exercise between the helper and the individual to assess what has been achieved, and to draw the process to a conclusion. Endings can be difficult, and the helper needs to use his or her skills to ensure that this is a positive time characterized by a sense of personal growth.

Maria. Maria had been seeing the liaison nurse for about three months. The time between their meetings began to lengthen and the meetings were increasingly being taken up with more general discussions. The nurse felt that it was time to evaluate outcome and to draw the process to a conclusion, so they agreed to set aside the next session for this evaluation. Because she had made note of the aims after the early sessions, she was able to remind them both of the original aims that they had set, and asked Maria to think about what had or had not been achieved. She suggested that Maria write this down at home and bring it to the next session.

The nurse encouraged Maria to lead the session by describing the aims and saying to what extent she thought they had been met, thus helping Maria to feel more in control and in need of less help. It was a tangible way of acknowledging Maria's own increasing sense of confidence in herself. Maria identified one long-term aim which had been set, that of being able to lead a more active social life. In order to achieve that aim, there had been a short-term aim of identifying the problems, and a medium-term aim of developing strategies to deal with social situations. Maria said that she felt that she had fully identified the problems, so the short-term aim had been met. She felt that she had developed some coping strategies which helped her, although there was still some way to go. However, she did say that she felt she now understood what to do and could do this by herself. Thus the medium-term aim had been partially met, but did not need active help from the nurse to complete. The long-term aim remained more elusive, as Maria still found social situations difficult at times, and had to work hard at them. However, she felt she was making progress towards this, and had a sense of optimism that this progress would continue. She recognized that there might always be some tension in social situations, and thus that the long-term aim would not be completely met, but she did feel that she no longer avoided such situations, and did have a greater sense of social freedom.

Decisions about concluding the helping process came from Maria. Having evaluated the outcome, she was able to say that while she was grateful for the help she had received, she felt that she could now manage by herself. The helper encouraged this and expressed the feeling that Maria had worked hard to achieve what she had, and that she admired her courage in a difficult situation. Because this reflected the reality of their work together and because of the warmth of their relationship, this was a genuine emotion, and perceived by Maria as such. The belief that she had played a major role in her progress was important to her, and increased her sense of optimism and personal efficacy. She was able to move on and needed no further help.

John. The ending of the helping relationship between the OT and John was more abrupt. Although John had agreed to participate, it had been for the sake of his girlfriend and he had never been really comfortable attending. He returned to work earlier than anticipated, which did not allow time to evaluate outcome and draw things to a conclusion. In the initial contract, they had agreed that they would work together until he went back to work, which was in itself an aim of helping. However, the OT had not planned the ending of the process. He felt dissatisfied as it had seemed too abrupt, but John did not attend a follow-up appointment. Even though the initial contract may specify when the process will end, it should also include some agreement as to *how* it would end. The helper was left unsure about final outcome, while John felt that although the process seemed helpful, it was something he needed to get away from. In such cases the individual may well be resistant to further help should the need arise.

Julie. It can be particularly difficult to draw the helping process to an end for someone like Julie who has suffered severe disfiguring injuries and who may develop different psychological problems as she grows up. For such people, the helper needs to recognize that there needs to be a long-term 'safety net' which can be used as needed. However, it would be wrong to professionalize her life by providing professional help which did not allow normal social support patterns to develop.

In Julie's case, there was no evaluation of final outcome because of the long-term issue. Instead, the social worker used times of transition such as changing of schools and leaving school to look at what had been achieved, and what, if anything, needed to be done. When he was not actively engaged in helping Julie through a specific difficulty, such as her return to school, then he withdrew and made no effort to contact her. He found this difficult as he was worried about her, but he needed to be able to trust her and her family to cope, and trust that they would initiate any contact. He had worked with Julie's mother and sister to help them to resume a more normal family life, and had been instrumental in helping Julie to have a more active social life. Thus he encouraged normal patterns of social relationships.

Andrew and Tracy. For Andrew and Tracy, the evaluation of outcome and the ending of the helping process was the most important element of the whole interaction. The health visitor felt that the time had come for this when they had started to communicate between themselves about their feelings and were both actively involved in the helping process. She arranged that the next time they met, they would discuss together how far they had come and what further role, if any, she had as a helper. This gave them the opportunity to talk together about this prior to the session and further encouraged their communication.

At the meeting, the health visitor encouraged Andrew and Tracy to talk together about their progress. This developed into a discussion between the two of them in which her role was simply to listen. She was able to reflect back to them that they seemed much more self-confident as parents and could make their own judgements now about what to do. She also reflected her sense that they were now talking about Jonathan more as a little boy who happened to have a mark, rather than talking just about the mark. She was able to accurately make these observations because she had observed their progress and had listened carefully to what they were saying. They were left with the sense that the progress was *their* achievement, and although they thanked her for her time, felt that they had played the major part in what had happened. The helper saw their reactions as an indication of the usefulness of the helping process; it had empowered them and did not create a grateful dependency. They agreed to end the meetings and did not arrange any further contact.

Conclusions

This chapter has described in some detail ways in which the helper can work with individuals with disfigurement and their families in order to facilitate their ability to cope with the disfigurement. In order for strategies to be useful, they must be linked closely to individual needs and to the agreed aims. There are common problems experienced by families and individuals, and ways of helping have been described within the context of these problems. However, each individual has their own unique personality, support system and ability to cope. The most important factor in any helping process is the quality of the relationship that has been developed between the individual and the helper, and it is in the context of that relationship that the individual will feel safe to reveal him or herself, and develop the confidence to cope.

SUMMARY

❏ There are many ways in which the helper can use his or her skills to facilitate change for someone with disfigurement. The type of help should relate to the problems, the aims and to the individual's reactions and resources.

❏ The following techniques and strategies were described in this chaper.

Coping with social encounters: controlling stress, developing a script, positive ignoring and distraction, dealing with awkward or hostile strangers, learning to use the force-field, modifying thoughts and beliefs, coping with teasing.

Coping with disruption to normal life: re-entry to school following trauma, returning to work using behavioural methods.

Coping with body image problems: desensitization to the disfigured part, coping with the reactions of others, allowing distress and anger to be expressed, ways of handling sexual problems.

Coping with treatment: making decisions about treatment, getting through difficult treatment, finding alternatives to physical treatment.

Coping with post-traumatic symptoms: normalizing the experience and re-evaluating beliefs about the world.

Coping with adjustment to the birth: bereavement counselling, facilitating communication between the parents, developing ways of coping with others.

Coping with the reactions of family and friends: talking with other family members, referring on to other agencies.

❏ At times, the problem cannot be solved, but can be managed so that the person emerges feeling emotionally stronger. Coping with loss requires a holding relationship in which distress can be experienced and the person can feel safe to express their worst emotions.

❏ The individual needs to be able to accept him or herself, however altered, before he or she can truly cope with the reactions of others.

❏ Evaluation of progress and outcome leads logically to concluding the helping process. This is an important time which allows the process to move from professionalization to normalization.

8

Conclusions: Helping the Helper

People with visible disfigurement may experience problems which relate to social perceptions of disfigurement and to their own psychological needs. Those who are close to them, including helpers, may also be affected by their disfigurement and sometimes they need help as well. This book is intended to give guidelines to those who wish to help, but lack experience and knowledge in this field. However, all helpers, even the most experienced, require training and supervision to make the best use of their skills. There are several ways in which you can develop support for your work:

1) through regular supervision;
2) through further education and training;
3) through contact with support groups.

Supervision

The emotional impact of disfigurement has already been discussed. It can provoke powerful reactions, stemming from psychological, social and cultural forces, and the person working with someone with disfigurement is not immune to these reactions. Indeed, if he or she felt no reaction to a serious facial burn or to a child with a craniofacial condition then they would be experiencing what has been termed by war photographers as 'the anaesthetic of familiarity'. In other words, regular contact with disfigurement can numb the person to its impact.

It is important to remain sensitive to disfigurement. This allows you to understand its effect on the person with whom you are working and/or the people in the street. It makes you a more effective helper as it increases your ability to empathize with those you are helping – you have not closed yourself defensively but remain open to them. However, it also renders you vulnerable to an emotional burden of subjective distress. Nurses working in trauma units often experience 'burn-out', when they suffer stress-related illness because of the emotional strain of the work.

To cope with this problem and remain a sensitive helper, you need to establish regular supervision. Good supervision can serve other purposes; it can offer professional support to help you evaluate what you are doing and to modify your approach on the basis of that evaluation, thus helping you improve your effectiveness as a helper. This is particularly important if you are new to this work and/or if the work does not fall within your usual pattern of professional activity. For example, a physiotherapist who is working with someone's emotional needs may find that the normal avenues of professional support do not include this type of work.

Supervision can take many forms. In some professions, such as social work, supervision is built into the professional structure. However, other professionals have no organized means of obtaining this supervision and it will need to be arranged informally. This requires you to approach someone whom you recognize as a potential supervisor and to negotiate some time for this.

Choosing a supervisor. Who would make a good supervisor? The person does not need experience in the field of disfigurement – it is unlikely that you would find a person with such experience. However, they should have experience of working with people who have psychological problems, and they should have an interest in the type of work you are doing. In addition, you should feel that they are approachable, that they can listen effectively and they can facilitate your helping skills. In other words, your supervisor should have the qualities of a good helper.

Timing. The timing of supervision will always be a matter of negotiation and expediency. Each session should last long enough to give you time to describe your work with at least one person and to allow for discussion about how you are coping with the situation. You will generally find that your supervision sessions should last about an hour. It helps if you prepare for these sessions and make notes to take with you, as this allows a more effective use of the time.

Just as with those you are helping, the purpose of the supervision is not to take over your work but to empower you to do it more effectively. There should be time between sessions for you to assimilate what you have learned and experienced.

Individual supervision sessions

A supervision session should include:

* *case discussion* – you should be prepared to discuss at least one person

with whom you are working. Make notes and consider where you need advice and guidance.

- *evaluation of outcome* – this should be an on-going exercise, not one that is limited to a retrospective analysis. It requires you to note the aims that have been established and the extent to which these aims have been met. It is not sufficient that you feel they have been met, the person with whom you are working should feel that progress is being made. Sometimes change can prove elusive and the process can become discouraging as you feel you have achieved nothing. The supervisor should be able to help you identify why this might be happening and how you can improve your helping skills to move forward.

- *discussion of the helper's emotional responses to the helping work* – this is not always necessary, but there should be time for it as it is an important component of supervision. By encouraging this dialogue, the supervisor can offer support to the helper and can ensure that the helper's emotional reactions are not hidden but are used to increase an understanding of the helping process. Some people may need permission to talk about their own reactions and may not see them as relevant or may be rather ashamed of them. This can be particularly true for professionals, such as surgeons, who are traditionally discouraged from discussing their emotions within a professional setting.

Confidentiality. Just as the helping process is confidential, so the supervision session should be confidential. However, the person with disfigurement who is being discussed should be aware that this will be taking place. This helps to ensure that such a person is aware of any discussion about them and is told the outcome of such a discussion.

Supervision groups

Sometimes supervision can work effectively in staff groups. Staff working in burns units for example, or in intensive care units, may benefit greatly from a sharing of concerns and a pooling of expertise. Such groups can be led by an experienced person with professional expertise in psychology, psychiatry or a related discipline. The benefit of such groups is that they allow staff to support each other and to recognize that they are not alone in their emotional reactions. Varying levels of experience within the group can be helpful in offering advice and experience in working with people with disfigurement and their families. The group experience can be structured by suggesting that individual cases are discussed. The disadvantage of such groups is that it does not allow an individual to explore his or her emotions in a confidential way, and some people find that difficult to do in a group setting. There is also less focus on the helper's individual work and more general discussion.

It could be that both individual and group sessions are of benefit, and can be combined effectively in a programme of supervision.

Education and Training

Once you have started this work, you may feel that you would benefit from further training to enable you to improve your helping skills. General training is more easy to obtain than specific training in the area of disfigurement, and there are many courses, both full-time and part-time, which offer counselling skills. It is important that you ensure that the course is run by a bona fide organization, and if you wish to practise as a counsellor, you will need to ensure that any qualifications you obtain accredit you for such work. A list of relevant organizations to approach for further details can be found at the back of this book.

Further training in the field of facial disfigurement is much more elusive. It is a specialized area and you will need to search for it. Journals such as *The Psychologist* and *The Nursing Times* sometimes give details of relevant courses. If you have a particular interest in this area and want to develop it further, it is worth contacting psychologists and counsellors already working with people with disfigurement in order to arrange visits to discuss and observe. These professionals can often be contacted through plastic surgery units, burns units or craniofacial units.

Another important means of increasing your knowledge is through reading relevant literature. The reference list at the end of this book contains some useful articles and books covering different aspects of disfigurement. Further literature can be accessed through the computer network in medical and university libraries. It is important to keep up-to-date with new work in this rapidly developing field.

Support Groups

There are many support groups which are organized by people with different types of disfigurement and their families. The purpose of these groups ranges from offering mutual support to campaigning for political change. Some groups are highly structured and run by committees who organize fund-raising, talks by professionals, research, social activities and public campaigns. Others are networks of interested people who get in contact with each other on an individual basis. Further details of all these groups can be found at the end of this book.

These support groups are intended for those who have the disfiguring condition and their families, but they can also be of great value for the helper. They provide information about the condition and the opportunity to meet and talk with people who have their own experience to offer. The helper should have the details of such organizations in order to give information to others when this is relevant, but should also bear in mind that not everyone will want to have contact with support groups.

The aim of this book has been to give you the confidence to help those with disfigurement. There are no certainties in this work, just the knowledge that you are doing your best to understand the problems and to understand the individual who is struggling with these problems. That person is the expert on his or her situation, but may need your help to turn that expertise into effective coping.

SUMMARY

❑ Working in this field can be very stressful as the helper may be helping those with serious injuries or upsetting disfiguring conditions. The helper may react in a personal way to this.

❑ The work can also seem specialized and the helper may feel a lack of specialist skills.

❑ The helper can be helped by supervision and by further training.

❑ Supervision sessions can be on an individual or a group basis, and should include discussion of cases as well as allowing the helper to express personal reactions.

❑ Training should be on-going and responsive to need. It can be to improve general helping skills or to learn specialist techniques. It should be through accredited organizations.

❑ Support groups can be useful for the individual, and the helper may also benefit and have something to offer such groups.

❑ Support groups vary widely in their activities, from regular meetings to occasional newsletters, and from political activity to mutual support. Many of the larger groups encompass all these activities.

Appendix A: Support Groups (UK)

Acne Support Group, 16 Dufours Place, Broadwick St, London W1, UK. Provides up-to-date information about acne and rosacea, and has a newsletter. Founded by Dr Tony Chu, a dermatologist, in 1993.

BACUP, 3 Bath Place, Rivington St, London EC2A 3JA, UK. Tel: Info: 0800 181199 or 0171 613 2121; Counselling: 0171 696 9000. Provides professional information by phone and leaflet on many aspects of cancer, and has a counselling service for those who can reach its base. Founded in the early 1980s by Dr Vicki Clement-Jones, a GP who later died of cancer.

Cancerlink, 17 Britannia Place, London WC1X 9JN, UK. Tel: 0171 833 2451. Provides information and networking for groups and individuals affected by cancer; runs courses and workshops on all aspects of cancer care and self-help.

Changing Faces, 27 Cowper St, London EC2A 4AP, UK. Tel: 0171 251 4232. Provides information and advice, counselling and social skills workshops in London and around Britain for anyone affected by facial disfigurement whatever the cause. Founded by James Partridge, a burns survivor, in 1992.

Cleft Lip and Palate Association (CLAPA), Co-ordinator: Mrs Cy Thirlaway, 1 Eastwood Gardens, Kenton, Newcastle upon Tyne, UK. Tel: 0191 285 9396. For children with cleft lip and/or palate and their families. Has a national network of local parent-support groups and provides supportive literature and aids to help with feeding etc. Founded by staff at Great Ormond Street Hospital.

Cranio-Facial Support Group, Trem Hafren, Earlswood, Chepstow, Gwent NP6 6AN, UK. Tel: 01291 641547. Established in 1994 to provide a network of families with craniofacial conditions such as Apert's and Crouzon's syndromes.

Cystic Hygroma Support Group, c/o Mrs Pearl Fowler, Villa Fontana, Church Road, Crawley, W Sussex, UK. Tel: 01293 885901. Provides information about the condition and contact with other families; organizes an all-day meeting once a year.

Disfigurement Guidance Centre, PO Box 7, Cupar, Fife KY15 4PF, UK. Tel: 0133 331 2350. Provides information and advice, especially concerning birthmarks, and raises money for laser therapy via the charity, Laserfair. Founded in the 1960s by Doreen Trust who has a portwine stain.

Dystrophic Epidermolysis Bullosa Research Association (DEBRA), 1 Kings Road, Crowthorne, Berks RG11 7BG, UK. Tel: 01344 771961. Provides information and newsletters, has full-time support nurses and raises funds for medical research.

Let's Face It, 10 Wood End, Crowthorne, Berks, UK. Tel: 01344 774405. Provides a support network around the UK and in other countries for those with facial disfigurements, especially after cancer treatment; has a summer garden party. Founded by Christine Piff in 1983 after her experience of facial cancer. Regular newsletter.

Lupus UK, PO Box 999, Romford, Essex RM1 1DW, UK. Tel: 01708 731251. Provides support and contact through local groups, advice and information as well as organizing educational meetings.

Naevus Support Group, 58 Necton Road, Wheathampstead, St Albans, Herts, UK. Tel: 01582 832853. Provides information about all forms of birthmark and a support network of parents meets twice a year. Founded and run by Renate and John O'Neill.

National Eczema Society, 4 Tavistock Place, London WC1H 9RA, UK. Tel: 0171 388 4097. Provides information and advice on many aspects of eczema for parents and professionals; campaigns for more resources within the NHS and has educational aims.

Neurofibromatosis Association (LINK), 120 London Road, Kingston on Thames, Surrey, KT2 6QJ, UK. Tel: 0181 547 1636. Information, contact with other parents, support and advice; newsletter and meetings.

The Psoriasis Association, 7 Milton St, Northampton NN2 7JG, UK. Tel: 01604 711129. Provides a range of information leaflets, newsletters, help and advice, and has regional groups around the country.

REACH, c/o Sue Stokes, 12 Wilson Way, Earls Barton, Northamptonshire NN6 0NZ, UK. Tel: 01604 811 041. Set up by a group of parents whose children had congenital limb deficiency due to Thalidomide. Provides information and support to families of children with congenital limb problems. A national organization with local branches. Organizes regular social and educational events, and funds research.

Sturge-Weber Foundation (UK), c/o Lynn Buchanan, 53 Brooklands Road West, Old Swan, Liverpool, L13 2BG, UK. Tel: 0151 220 5290. Provides support, information and advice to families affected by the condition and has an annual family conference.

Treacher-Collins Family Support Group, c/o Sue Moore, 114 Vincent Road, Thorpe Hamlet, Norwich, Norfolk NR1 4HH, UK. Tel: 01603 33736. Provides support, friendship, information and advice on this condition as well as Nager syndrome, and First and Second Arch syndrome.

The Vitiligo Society, PO Box 919, London SE21 8AW, UK. Tel: 0181 776 7022. Provides support and advice, a regular newsletter and holds meetings to which professionals are invited; also sponsors medical research.

Other Groups

The Guinea Pig Club, c/o Queen Victoria Hospital, East Grinstead, UK. This is for Second World War veterans who received pioneering plastic surgery at East Grinstead after the war.

National Association of Laryngectomy Clubs, 39 Eccleston Square, London SW1, UK.

Red Cross Society – Cosmetic Camouflage Service, Grosvenor Terrace, London W1, UK.

Appendix B: Support Groups (USA)

About Face – USA, PO Box 93, Lime Kiln, Pennsylvania 19535, USA. Tel: (800) 225 3223. Program to teach school children about facial differences; outreach program to individuals and families affected by facial differences.

American Cancer Society, 1599 Clifton Road NE Atlanta, Georgia 30329–4251, USA. Tel: (800) 227 2345. Provide information and networking for individuals who have cancer.

Association of Birth Defect Children, 827 Irma Avenue, Orlando, Florida 32803, USA. Tel: (407) 245 7035. Serves as a clearinghouse to provide free information about birth defects; sponsors National Birth Defects Registry, and matches parents by children's birth defects.

Candlelighters Childhood Cancer Foundation, 7910 Woodmont Avenue, Suite 460, Bethesda, Maryland 20814, USA. Tel: (800) 366 2223. Provides education, support groups information, and advocacy for children who have cancer and their families.

Cleft Palate Foundation, 1218 Grandview Avenue, Pittsburgh, Pennsylvania 15211, USA. Tel: (800) 242 5338. Professional association that provides information and referrals on cleft palate.

DEBRA: Dystrophic Epidermolysis Bullosa Research Association, 40 Rector Street, New York, NY 10006, USA. Tel: (212) 693 6610. Offers information, newsletters, and networking.

FACES: National Association for the Craniofacially Handicapped, PO Box 11082, Chattanooga, Tennessee 37401, USA. Tel: (800) 332 2373. Assists with expenses for families who need to travel for medical care; provides information and networking for people with craniofacial disorders.

National Neurofibromatosis Foundation, 95 Pine Street, 16th Floor, New York, NY 10005, USA. Tel: (800) 323 7938. Provides information for families of persons with neurofibromatosis and helps raise money for research.

National Psoriasis Foundation, 6600 SW 92nd, Suite 300 Portland, Oregon 97223, USA. Tel: (503) 244 7404. A voluntary, member-supported lay health organization with a mission of psoriasis research and education.

Sturge-Weber Foundation, PO Box 418, Mt. Freedom, New Jersey 07970, USA. Tel: (800) 627 5482. Clearinghouse for parents and professionals; provides information, networking, advocacy, parent counselling, and research funding worldwide.

References

Benson, B. A., Gross, A. M., Messer, S. C., Kellum, G. and Passmore, L. A. (1991) Social support network among families of children with craniofacial anomalies. *Health Psychology, 10(4)*, 252–258.

Bettleheim, B. (1972) How do you help a child who has a physical handicap? *Ladies Home Journal, 89*, 34.

Bradbury, E. T. and Kay, S. P. J. (1990) 'Now I'm Somebody Special'. *British Medical Journal, 302*, 879.

Bradbury, E. T., Hewison, J. and Timmons, M. J. (1992) Psychological and social outcome of prominent ear correction in children. *British Journal of Plastic Surgery, 45*, 97–100.

Bradbury, E.T. and Hewison, J. (1994a) Early parental responses to visible congenital anomalies. *Child; Care, Health and Development, 20*, 251–266.

Bradbury, E. T., Kay, S. P. J., Tighe, C. T. and Hewison, J. (1994b) Decision-making by parents and children in paediatric hand surgery. *British Journal of Plastic Surgery, 47*, 324–330.

Bradbury, E. T., Kay, S. P. J., and Hewison, J. (1994c) The psychological impact of microvascular free toe transfer for children and their parents. *Journal of Hand Surgery (British and European Volume), 19B; 6*, 689–695.

Bull, R. and Rumsey, N. (1988). *The Social Psychology of Facial Appearance*. New York: Springer-Verlag.

Crockenberg, S. (1981) Infant irritability, mother responsiveness, and social influences on the security of infant–mother attachment. *Child Development, 52*, 857–865.

Dion, K. K., Berscheid, E. and Walster, E. (1972) What is beautiful is good. *Journal of Personality and Social Psychology, 24*, 285–290.

Dion, K.K., and Berscheid, E. (1974) Physical attractiveness and peer perception among children. *Sociometry, 3(1)*, 1–12.

Field, T. M. and Vegha-Lahr, N. (1984) Early interactions between infants with craniofacial anomalies and their mothers. *Infant Behaviour and Development, 7*, 527–530.

Fisk, S. B., Pearl, R. M. Schulman, G. I. and Wong, H. (1985) Congenital facial anomalies among 4- through 7-year-olds: psychological effects and surgical decisions. *Annals of Plastic Surgery, 14(1)*, 37–42.

Fonagy, P., Steele, H and Steele, M. (1991) Intergenerational patterns of attachment: maternal representations of attachment during pregnancy and subsequent infant–mother attachment. *Child Development, 62*, 891–905.

Fonagy, P., Steele, M., Steele, H., Higgitt, A. and Target, M. (1994) The Emmanuel Miller Memorial Lecture 1992. The Theory and Practice of Resilience. *Journal Of Child Psychiatry and Psychology, 35(2)*, 231–257.

Fransella, F. and Dalton, P. (1990) *Personal Construct Counselling in Action*. London: Sage.

Goffman, E. (1963) *Stigma: notes on the management of spoiled identity*. Englewood Cliffs, New Jersey: Prentice-Hall Inc.

Goldberg, R. T. (1974) Adjustment of children with invisible and visible handicaps – congenital heart disease and facial burns. *Journal of Counselling Psychology, 21(5)*, 428–432.

Langlois, J. H., and Stephan, C. (1981) Beauty and the beast: the role of physical attractiveness in the development of peer relations and social behavior. In S. S. Brehm, S. M. Kassin, and F. X. Gibbons (Eds), *Developmental Social Psychology: theory and research*. New York: Oxford University Press.

Lansdown, R. (1990) Psychological problems of patients with cleft lip and palate: discussion paper. *Journal of Royal Society of Medicine, 83*, 448–450.

Lazarus, R. (1966) *Psychological Stress and the Coping Process*. New York: McGraw Hill.

Macgregor, F. C. (1982) Social and psychological studies of plastic surgery. *Clinics in Plastic Surgery, 9(3)*, 283–288.

Main, M., Kaplan, N. and Cassidy, J (1985) Security in infancy, childhood and adulthood: a move to the level of representation in T. Bretherton and E. Waters (Eds). Growing points in attachment theory and research. *Monogram of the Society for Research in Child Development, 50*, (1–2).

Olweus, D. (1993) *Bullying at school: What we know and what we can do*. Oxford: Blackwell.

Pastor, D. L. (1981) The quality of mother–infant attachment and its relationship to toddlers' initial sociability with peers. *Developmental Psychology, 17*, 326–335.

Pillemer, F. G. and Kaye, V. C. (1989) The psychosocial adjustment of paediatric craniofacial patients. *Cleft Palate Journal, 26(3)*, 201–208.

Rogers, C. (1959) A theory of therapy, personality and interpersonal relationships as developed in the client-centred framework. In S. Koch (Ed.) *Psychology: a study of a science*. New York: McGraw-Hill.

Rutter, M. and Rutter, M. (1992) *Developing Minds: Challenge and Continuity across the Life Span*. London: Penguin.

Seligman, M. E. P. (1975) *Helplessness*. San Francisco: Freeman.

Shaw W. C. (1981) Folklore surrounding facial deformity and the origins of facial prejudice. *British Journal of Plastic Surgery, 34*, 237–246.

Solnit, A. and Stark, M. H. (1962) Mourning and the birth of a defective child. *Psychoanalytic Study of the Child, 16*, 9–24.

Timberlake, E. M. (1985) Self-Concept Protection by Children with Physical Differences. *Child and Adolescent Social Work*, 233–245.

Index

Compiled by Frances Coogan